INCLUDING FAMILIES OF CHILDREN WITH SPECIAL NEEDS

A How-To-Do-It Manual For Librarians

Sandra Feinberg
Barbara Jordan
Kathleen Deerr
Michelle Langa

*HOW-TO-DO-IT MANUALS
FOR LIBRARIANS*

NUMBER 88

NEAL-SCHUMAN PUBLISHERS, INC.
New York, London

Published by Neal-Schuman Publishers, Inc.
100 Varick Street
New York, NY 10013

Printed and bound in the United States of America.

Library of Congress Cataloging-in-Publication Data

Feinberg, Sandra, 1946–
        Including families of children with special needs / Sandra
Feinberg . . . [et al.].
        p. cm. — (How-to-do-it manuals for librarians : no. 88)
Includes bibliographical references and index.
ISBN 1-55570-339-9
        1. Libraries and handicapped children—United States. 2.
Libraries—Services to families—United States. 3.
Libraries—Services to preschool children—United States. I. Title.
II. Series: How-to-do-it manuals for libraries : no. 88.
        Z711.92.H3 F45 1999
        027.6'63—ddc21   98-48982
                                                                        CIP

DEDICATION

This book is dedicated to our families: Richie, Jake, and Teddy; Fred, Courtney, and Eric; Al, A.J., and David; and Frank and Zach, who did without us so much of the time during the creation of this work. Thanks for your support, understanding, and good humor.

CONTENTS

PREFACE

Prior to 1986, children with disabilities were often placed in segregated, special education settings or were confined to the home without any participation in community life. This pattern is gradually changing. Since the passage of Part C (formerly known as Part H) of the Individuals with Disabilities Education Act, the special education field has been striving for inclusion of young children (birth to five years) and their families within the community. This emphasis on community life experience allows libraries to be partners in the process.

The principle of inclusion maintains that children with disabilities should not be confined to separate facilities and programs, but rather they have the right to participate in typical community settings together with children without disabilities. It is based on the recognition that all children have needs, strengths, and something to contribute and that every child needs some form of accommodation. These commonalties outweigh any differences between children with "special needs" and others.

Including Families of Children with Special Needs: A How-To-Do It Manual for Librarians focuses on families with children up to age five. It covers the basic principles underlying inclusion, family-centered service, resource-based practice, and the provision of library service to families and children with special needs. This manual has a practical bias, and the outlined strategies and methods focus on communication skills, competencies, adaptations, collaborations, networks, training, programs, and collection development.

We wrote this manual because it is not enough for librarians just to *say* that libraries are welcoming and accessible or that their programs and services are not restrictive. Librarians must take a proactive stance to include families of children with special needs in programs and services; they must develop strategies to seek out opportunities to reach these families. Certain basic attributes make libraries ideal community places for families and children with special needs. Libraries are well-established local institutions available in almost every community that offer a nonjudgmental, safe, nonthreatening, and comfortable environment for community residents. They are accessible year-round, most often with extended hours of operation during evenings and weekends. They are information centers with trained staff and established collections that serve both parents and children and often offer programs and services for these audiences. Libraries provide a connecting link between families and other community agencies.

Most library service to children is not restricted. There are no "official" barriers or rules that bar children from the library. However, not everyone perceives the library as an open place. Often parents of young children are influenced and intimidated by stereotypes such as the "shushing" librarian, the mistaken notion that use of the library requires the ability to read, or the feeling that libraries are not for young children who are noisy and active. Consequently, many parents may not bring their young children to the library. If their children have disabilities, the perceived barriers may be even more daunting. How can the library serve these children?

INCLUDING THEIR CHILDREN

Librarians who read this book will be ready to begin the process of including children with special needs and their families in regular library programming. They will not only have the philosophical framework, but also the practical knowledge needed to give high-quality service to children with a variety of disabilities. Other readers will be prepared to work with librarians after gaining an understanding of how the library plays a pivotal role in the development of all children, including those with disabilities.

Including Families of Children with Special Needs can help any library develop or improve their own services to this important population. The first four chapters define the policies and practices underlying an inclusive institution. Chapter 1 covers inclusion and the benefits of inclusion for all families and the public library. Anecdotes and stories give librarians a realistic picture of how inclusion improves library service and an understanding of why libraries need to get involved in serving families of children with special needs.

Chapter 2 outlines the laws and regulations that support inclusion, including relevant sections of the Individuals with Disabilities Act and the Americans with Disabilities Act. Special mention is also given to the National Education Goals: America 2000 Act.

Chapters 3 and 4 address principles of family-centered service and resource-based practice. These include the importance of developmentally appropriate services for children under five years, the family's influence in the lives of young children, the wisdom of the library's serving as a "natural" environment, and the roles of the librarian in providing service to families and children with special needs.

Chapter 5 focuses on assessing the readiness of the library, particularly the children's services department, to include children with special needs and their families. The exploration of personal attitudes about children with disabilities, the role of the library in the inclusion process, competencies and skills for librarians, and a checklist of appropriate terms to use with families are included. These steps and strategies to prepare for inclusion will assist staff in their efforts to educate and inform themselves.

Chapters 6 and 7 focus on communication and outreach: understanding the needs of parents whose children have disabilities, sensitivity issues, and communication skills, along with practical strategies for reaching out to parents. If librarians want to develop inclusive services it is essential that they build them collaboratively with parents as well as with early intervention and preschool special education professionals. The list of competencies and skills for effective collaboration (page 74) and examples of collaborative efforts will help in the planning process.

Chapters 8 and 9 provide program and collection guidelines, either for adaptations of existing programs or the initiation of new services. Adaptations of typical library programs and services, birth through age five, are brought to life through anecdotes and stories based on "real" experiences.

Chapter 10 examines the importance of play and the availability of appropriate toys in the development of young children. Librarians share their expertise and practical experience in establishing an inclusive toy-lending library with reference to LEKOTEK, a national model toy-lending "library."

Resources for parents and professionals, an essential element of quality library service to families and children with special needs, are covered in Chapters 11 and 12. A brief overview of Internet resources for parents and professionals who work with children with disabilities, with special emphasis on sites that provide supportive "chat groups" for adults and children, is also provided.

The appendices include an extensive bibliography on inclusion, a developmental milestone checklist, a state-by-state listing of early intervention program coordinators for Part C of the Individuals with Disabilities Education Act, and a description of Parent Resource Centers in Public Libraries, an initiative developed by the Developmental Disabilities Planning Council (New York State).

Welcoming families and children with disabilities into our libraries and creating new services or adapting existing services for children with special needs is not just a trendy phase. Children have always selected resources and activities at the public library based on individual interests and situations. Children with disabilities have these same needs, and they have a right to these same choices. Unless children with disabilities are proactively included they may, in practice, be excluded. It is incumbent upon the librarian to develop a greater understanding of disabling conditions, be sensitive to the needs of families, ensure that children with special needs are welcomed and served, and effect the change needed to create an inclusive atmosphere in the library setting.

Providing services to children with special needs requires skills and an understanding beyond the traditional service role of the public librarian. It stretches the institution and the staff, requiring an assessment of attitudes about differences and a concerted effort to reach out and include new communities within the library setting. To include children with disabilities, children's librarians not only have to be comfortable with young children in general, but with children who have special needs and with their families. *Including Families of Children with Special Needs* is designed to insure that the principle of inclusion becomes a reality. Although we address children's librarians, outreach librarians, and library administrators, our hope is that early intervention and family support professionals, early childhood educators, childcare workers, family home daycare providers, and policy makers who work with and for children with special needs and their families will also find the information in this manual useful.

CONTRIBUTORS

Special recognition is given to the professional listed below for contributing their expertise and authorship. Their knowledge and commitment to services for families and children with disabilities are exemplary and greatly appreciated by the families and professionals with whom they work. Our manuscript is more valuable because of their willingness to share their expertise.

Chapter 10

Rachel Catan, Mastics-Moriches-Shirley Community Library

Lois Eannel, Middle Country Public Library

Virginia Reed Maloney and Susan J. Oliver, National Lekotek Center

Chapter 11 and Appendix D

Anna Lobosco, New York State Developmental Disabilities Planning Council

ACKNOWLEDGMENTS

Thanks are extended to Lorianne Hoenninger of the Association for Children with Learning and Developmental Disabilities, Julie Klauber of the Suffolk Cooperative Library System, and Colleen Moseman of the Long Island Toy Lending Center for Children With Disabilities for sharing their resources and expertise.

Recognition is also extended to those involved in the Partners for Inclusion Project (Suffolk County, N.Y., 1993–1995) which provided the basis for so much of the work represented in this book. Among those in the project are the staff of the Middle Country Public Library (Centereach, N.Y.), especially Lois Eannel, Mary Schumacher, Ellen Friedman, Doreen Holmes, and Carolyn Liljequist; the staff of the Mastic-Moriches-Shirley Community Library (Shirley, N.Y.), especially Rachel Catan and Eileen Curtin; project coordinators Noreen Buckhout and Ellen Paige Horst; Steve Held, Christine Clarke, Tom McMath, Barbara Morgan-Salvador, Amy Toole, and Amira Simha-Alpern of Just Kids Early Childhood Learning Center (Middle Island, N.Y.); Ellen Woodward, Joan Smart, Tina Malone, and Patricia Davison of Starting Early, Developmental Disabilities Institute (Selden, N.Y.); Janice Orland and Barbara Ross of the Bureau of Services for Children with Disabilities, Suffolk County Department of Health Services, as well as the many early intervention service providers who participated at various stages of the project; and to the New York State Department of Health, Bureau of Child and Adolescent Health, particularly Donna Noyes, Wendy Shaw, and Dan Frering. Their collaborative efforts resulted in positive change and enhancement of library-based services to the families and children with special needs that reside in these library communities.

We are especially grateful to Margaret Sampson for her personal and professional contributions to our understanding of the parents' perspective and her friendship, support, and encouragement of all our efforts on behalf of families. A special thanks is extended to the families and children with special needs who live in the Middle Country and Mastics-Moriches-Shirley communities for their willingness to share their experiences and work with us to educate ourselves and our communities regarding the issues they face on a daily basis. Without their participation, this book would not have been written.

PART I:
UNDERSTANDING
INCLUSIVE PRACTICES

1 WHAT'S INCLUSION ALL ABOUT?

Take a moment to observe young children in the library. They watch each other as often as they look at books. They talk to other children or adults in the picture book area, interact with staff in a story hour or at the circulation desk, and play with unfamiliar children during a program. They form attachments and make new friends. Children are, by nature, social creatures. They need to play with and observe peers. Being part of a group is almost as important as their need to eat or sleep. Simply put, children want to be included with other children. For children with disabilities, this need is often unfulfilled.

Children with disabilities are often set apart from their typically developing peers because of their "special needs." They are denied, in many situations, the opportunity to grow and learn from friends in their neighborhood, schools, and other community settings. When they become adults, having been educated in segregated special education classrooms or out-of-state residential schools, these children (and their families) continue to be isolated within their communities.

This kind of segregation and isolation is detrimental not only for families and children but for the society as a whole. An inclusionary philosophy recognizes that children have more things in common than not; all children have needs and strengths and can make contributions; and all children need some form of accommodation. Keeping children with disabilities apart from their typically developing peers only creates bigger problems later in life and fails to take advantage of the wonderful openness of young children to new experiences and their nonjudgmental attitude toward differences. Inclusion and opportunities for typical social experiences during the early years is critical for the healthy development of *all* children.

DEFINITION OF INCLUSION

Inclusion, as a philosophy and a national movement, reflects the efforts of parents and professionals trying to reverse the isolation experienced by those with disabilities. What is the meaning of inclusion? In humanitarian terms, inclusion is a welcoming, a celebration of diverse abilities, a profound respect for the contributions all children can make. It is a belief that communities of diversity are richer, better, and more productive places in which to live. Inclusive communities have the capacity to create a future that allows a better life for everyone.

In the legal sense, inclusion is a term that advocates that children, regardless of their diverse abilities, have the right to participate, and will benefit from participation, in typical community settings where children without disabilities are found. It supports families of children with special needs and their efforts to join in community life, have access to unbiased information, and participate fully in the decisions surrounding the education of their child. Inclusion encourages the child with a disability to participate in playground activities, child care settings, nursery schools or kindergarten programs, and activities at the local public library.

Inclusion, as a national movement, encompasses the humanitarian and legal perspective but the most compelling expression of inclusion is the fulfillment of a child's desire to have a friend and be accepted and valued as an individual. For families of children with special needs, this is a priority.

BENEFITS OF INCLUSION

An individual's prerogative to participate in activities and have access to resources is a basic tenet of library service. Inclusion expands on this principle by encouraging librarians to welcome diversity within the library environment and adapt services based on individual need. As with any group of library patrons, children with special needs and their families may or may not want to be included in all library programs. The principle of inclusion means that librarians will make it possible for any child, with or without a disability, to participate in library service.

Inclusion benefits not only families and children with disabilities but those families and children without disabilities who participate in an inclusive situation as well as the staff involved in making it happen. The following library vignettes, collected during parent focus groups (*Early Childhood Quality Review Initiative for Public Libraries*, 1995) and through individual parent interviews (Langa, 1996), help paint a picture of how inclusion works and what it looks like in the library.

BENEFITS FOR FAMILIES AND CHILDREN WITH DISABILITIES

Motivation to Gain or Practice Skills

The child with a disability benefits from playing with nondisabled peers because the interaction often motivates the child with disabilities to gain or practice needed skills. In addition, behavioral handicaps that are derived from social exclusion are often reduced or eliminated.

One little boy and his mom attended the library's early childhood programs from the time he was six weeks old. The boy was delayed in physical movement and needed to practice climbing steps with the physical therapist. His home did not have any accessible steps on which to practice and, because of their regular involvement in library programs, the mother knew the library's Early Childhood Room had a loft area with steps that were perfect to encourage this skill in her child. The mother approached the library staff to ask if the physical therapist could accompany the family to the library's workshop or meet at the library and practice step climbing. A time was selected that was convenient to the therapist and the family and which did not interfere with regular library service, and the therapist sometimes participated while the workshop was going on to really capitalize on helping the child in his normal environment.

A mom, whose son has Down's syndrome, related this story. Her son loved the ranch display in the children's museum corner, a special section of the library. Often, her child would spend his entire visit to the library with other children in this area. For the longest time after the display was taken down, her son would go back to the museum corner to see if he could find the horses. The mother was so pleased that her young son was able to remember the display and ask about the horses. He had made attachments and connections based on his library experience—an important step for him!

Increased Choices and Opportunities

The child with a disability has access to a greater range of choices and finds increased opportunities to develop language, social, and problem-solving skills when using the wide array of library programs, collections, and services for young children. For example, a mother of a hearing-impaired preschool child approached the children's librarian. She wondered if her preschooler could attend storytime and if the library would provide a sign language interpreter. This service was provided and the child was able to attend the storytime. She was introduced to a variety of books and finger plays, and interacted with the other children in the program, many of whom wanted to learn this special new way of "talking" too! The mother and child continue to participate in library programs and learning activities, working with the librarian to develop accommodations to make these experiences successful.

Through a collaborative program between the library and a local developmental disabilities school, an early intervention teacher became familiar with the library's services and asked if she could bring some children to storytime to enhance their language and social interaction skills. She and the librarian decided on the most appropriate storytime and, after attending storytime, these children brought their families back to select books and use the library on their own.

Opportunity for Friendships and Social Events

Families of children with disabilities find that they share common experiences, and they also have the opportunity to make friendships and participate in community events. One library had been working with several families in a program designed for children with special needs, held regularly at the library's branch. The library was celebrating its 35th anniversary at the main building and invited community members to an afternoon of activities including storytelling, singing groups, video viewings, and a puppet performance. During the afternoon, the director noticed three children in wheelchairs and their families excitedly entering the library to join the community celebration. These families had become well integrated into the life of their library. The warm welcome by the library staff, who had become so familiar with the families, added an extra level of enthusiasm to the festivities.

Source of Acceptance and Support

Families of children with special needs find that the library is a vital source of acceptance and support in the care of their children as well as access to unbiased information and resources.

During a Parent/Child Workshop (Feinberg and Deerr, 1995), the children's librarian noticed that one child did not seem to be verbalizing at all. The librarian engaged the mother in a discussion about the child's language development. The mother expressed a great deal of anxiety over her child's lack of speech. During the workshop series, a visiting speech therapist approached the mother at the request of the librarian. She gave a packet of information to the mother and told her about a center where she could take her child for testing. The mother did have the child tested and it was found that the child was experiencing a delay in language development. The mother was able to enroll the child in a special program. She came back to the librarian to express her thanks and seek out further information and resources about her child's disability. She also shared the difficulty her husband was having accepting the problem. The librarian gathered the information the mother needed about the child's speech delay and also located parenting books on raising a child with a special need that specifically discussed the acceptance issue. The mother was pleased to be able to pass on these books to her husband.

The mom of a child with a serious physical disability shared this story. She remembered having a casual conversation with a children's librarian regarding her child's equipment needs. Several weeks later, the librarian mailed her the catalog of an agency that deals with assistive technology for children with special needs. The parent stated that this extra effort was totally unexpected and reinforced her feeling that the library and the staff really had accepted her child and were genuinely concerned about his needs.

BENEFITS FOR FAMILIES AND CHILDREN WITHOUT DISABILITIES

Acceptance of Diverse Abilities

When inclusion is the norm for the library, children without disabilities learn at a young age to appreciate and accept the diverse abilities of all children. One mother described her child's wonderful imaginary play that reenacted her visits to the library. Her daughter played library at home, arranging books to be checked out. She organized activities with herself as teacher (librarian) and her dolls as attendees. The child read for friends, parents, and toys in attendance. The child even read to her dolls using sign language for those who were deaf!

Better Understanding of Disabilities

Families of children without disabilities gain greater understanding of disabilities, and they also develop a sense of pride in their children's natural ability to accept and appreciate differences in others. A parent focus group participant related that her child had learned to "behave and interact with others" and had also learned that "all children are not the same as her" after attending a library program that included children with special needs. The parent expressed pride in her child's acceptance of differences and was pleased that this opportunity was offered at the library.

BENEFITS OF INCLUSION FOR LIBRARIES AND LIBRARIANS

Impetus to Reexamine Library Practice

What works for children with disabilities and their families, works for others as well. Learning to adapt and identify ways to include children with special needs encourages us to examine rules, procedures, policies, facilities, programs, collections, and services. Improvements in service often benefit all patrons.

A library received a grant to develop a circulating toy collection for children with special needs, birth through age three. The children's librarian responsible for building the collection was excited about providing this new service. Toys arrived daily and were processed and made ready for circulation. A brochure was designed and a colorful notebook assembled. Just before the availability of the collection was announced to the public, the librarian thought about the child and parent checking the toy out at the circulation desk. How would other children feel? Wouldn't a child who wasn't qualified for the program want to check out such an attractive item? In fact, wouldn't the child with special needs stand out as "special" or "different"? The librarian approached the director and presented her dilemma, asking if it would be possible to purchase toys from the regular budget and allow all children to check out toys. The director agreed. Inclusion, in this instance, instigated the development of a new and exciting collection for all of the younger children in the community.

Expansion of User and Support Base

Inclusion offers an opportunity for libraries to widen the library's circle of users and supporters, while satisfying the needs of families and children with disabilities. When one library conducted parent focus groups, some of the most active participants were parents of children with special needs. They made suggestions such as streamlining registration procedures, relocating library suggestion boxes to elicit regular customer feedback, and conducting support groups for parents. These focus group parents became part of the library's regular user base and continue to interact with staff and administration on improvement of services. They brag to others, outside of the library district, about how supportive the library has been for their families. They are staunch library supporters and can be counted on to vote in the library's annual budget vote and trustee election.

Opportunities for Staff Development

Through experiences with families and children with special needs, library staff has an opportunity to increase their competencies and skills. One library, after reaching out to families and children with special needs, was overwhelmed at the response they received. The support staff expressed anxiety over how some of these children behaved in the library, and there was resistance that needed to be overcome. The head of the department realized that her staff needed skills on how to interact with these families and children and integrate them into the library environment. She contacted staff from the developmental disabilities school with which she was working. They provided a social worker who met with the library staff to sensitize them on issues surrounding families and children with disabilities. They discussed specific problems and designed practical solutions.

Welcoming families and children with disabilities into our libraries and creating new services or adapting existing services for children with special needs is not a fad. All children select resources and activities to participate in at the public library based on individual interests. Children with disabilities need and have a right to these same choices. The reality is that children with disabilities are either proactively included or they may, in practice, be excluded. It is incumbent upon the librarian to develop a greater understanding of disabling conditions, be sensitive to the needs of families, ensure that children with special needs are welcomed and served, and affect the change needed to create an inclusive atmosphere in the library setting.

REFERENCES

Early Childhood Quality Review Initiative for Public Libraries. 1995. Centereach, N.Y.: Middle Country Public Library.

Feinberg, Sandra and Kathleen Deerr. 1995. *Running a Parent/Child Workshop: A How-To-Do- It Manual for Librarians.* New York: Neal-Schuman.

Langa, Michelle. 1996. Notes from 1994 parent interviews. Centereach, N.Y.: Middle Country Public Library.

2 WHAT DOES THE LAW SAY?

In addition to a philosophical basis for providing services for children with special needs there is a legal impetus, which is outlined in the requirements of two federal laws: the Individuals with Disabilities Education Act (IDEA) and the Americans with Disabilities Act (ADA). These laws, as well as the educational goals for our nation that are outlined in the America 2000 Act, are designed to increase our awareness of diverse cultures and populations, increase the productivity of all members of society, eliminate discrimination based on differences, and ensure that *all* children enter school ready to learn.

It is not laws, however, that drive inclusion of children with disabilities in library services. It is the opportunity for librarians to assume the spirit of the law that is embodied in the fundamentals of good library service. Understanding the basic legal requirements and guidelines increases the librarian's understanding and knowledge of inclusion and should encourage more informed and appropriate implementation of inclusionary practice. How the law impacts on the practices of early intervention and preschool special education providers directly affects how librarians can work collaboratively with their community partners to include children with special needs and their families in the library setting.

THE INDIVIDUALS WITH DISABILITIES EDUCATION ACT (IDEA)

DEFINITION

IDEA is the federal law that ensures that all children (up to the age of 21) receive a free and appropriate education regardless of their disability. When first enacted, this law established legal definitions for children with specific learning disabilities and focused on children, preschool and up. It entitled eligible children to evaluations, special education, related services, an individual education program (IEP), transition services, and assistive technology. In 1986, Congress amended the law to include children three years old and younger. This amendment, originally listed as Part H of the Individuals with Disabilities Education Act, has recently been reauthorized as "Part C."

Part C defines infants and toddlers with disabilities as children under the age of three who need early intervention services because they are experiencing developmental delays in one or more of the following areas: cognitive development, physical development, language and speech development, psychosocial development, and self-help skills. The definition also includes children who have a diagnosed physical or mental condition that has a high probability of resulting in a developmental delay but may not be demonstrating that delay presently, for example, children with Down syndrome.

Part C states that early intervention services must be developmentally appropriate, provided under public supervision, and at no cost to families except where the state statute establishes a payment system for families based upon a sliding scale fee. These services can include family training, home visits and counseling, special instruction, speech pathology, audiology, occupational therapy, physical therapy, psychological services, medical services for diagnostic or evaluation purposes, social work services, vision services, and assistive technology devices and services.

For children up to the age of three, these services must be contained within an Individualized Family Service Plan (IFSP; see page 14) and be provided in a natural environment. This natural environment can be the child's home or a community setting in which children without disabilities typically participate. Outside of the home or child care situation, there are few natural or neutral settings available within the community that are appropriate for young children and their families. Public libraries are one of these settings. Inclusion supports the library's efforts to adapt the library's environment and encourages families and young children to make use of library resources.

Under Part B of IDEA, children aged three to five become the focus of intervention rather than the family. An Individualized Education Plan (IEP; see page 15) is developed rather than an IFSP. Services are no longer required to be provided in a natural setting but in the least restrictive one possible. This least restrictive environment mandate requires that, to the maximum extent appropriate, children with disabilities, including those in public or private institutions, are educated with children who are not disabled. According to this mandate, children with disabilities should only be removed from regular educational activities when the nature or severity of the child's disability is such that the child cannot satisfactorily achieve his or her educational goals even with the use of supplementary aids and services. A public library that offers programs for preschool children can serve as a least restrictive setting, helping to fulfill the requirements of the law.

ENTITLED SERVICES UNDER PART B AND PART C OF IDEA

Part B and Part C of IDEA establish the right of each child under five who is suspected of having a developmental disability to have access to certain services. These services include referral, service coordination, a multidisciplinary evaluation, an IFSP or IEP, and due process safeguards. Librarians who want to take the initiative can collaborate with early intervention providers, preschool special education personnel and parents in the implementation of the mandated services.

Referral

Infants, toddlers, or preschoolers suspected of having a developmental disability are entitled to a referral to the lead agency established within each state. This referral is the entry point for a child and family into the early intervention or preschool special education systems. Depending upon the state, referrals can be made by the parents themselves, family home or group day care providers, pediatricians, nurses, and other selected early childhood professionals. It is important for librarians to be aware of the referral process and understand how they can help to identify children who may be qualified for services. Librarians can

- familiarize themselves with their state's early intervention and preschool special education system's referral process;
- contact local service coordinators for networking and information purposes;
- provide information on disabilities and the referral processes for parents, family home day care providers, and early childhood professionals;
- gain knowledge about developmental milestones and, if a potential delay is recognized in the library setting, acquire skills on how to approach parents in a supportive manner;
- enhance communication skills in the provision of information and referral to parents.

Service Coordination

Under Part C, each family is entitled to service coordination to avoid duplication and fragmentation of early intervention services. Usually, a service coordinator is assigned by the lead agency or its designee shortly after a referral is made. Service coordination is a critical component of Part C. The service coordinator is responsible for

- obtaining information regarding the child and family that includes the child's health history and developmental status;
- obtaining permission to release medical and other records pertaining to the child's suspected delay;

- informing the family of the program and its rights under the state law;
- explaining the protections offered by the law regarding the family's health insurance;
- assisting the family in understanding and arranging for a screening or a multidisciplinary evaluation of the child;
- helping the family obtain answers to any questions they may have about the evaluation process and results;
- exploring with families of eligible children their options for services;
- explaining the IFSP and the family's primary role in developing and implementing that plan.

Under Part B, for children aged three to five, service coordination is handled by a member of the multidisciplinary team working with the child. Considering the change in focus from family to child, service coordination under Part B ensures that provided services are unduplicated, comprehensive, and dedicated to improving the child's academic performance as outlined in his/her IEP.

For librarians, what is important about service coordination is the recognition that parents, service coordinators, and members of the multidisciplinary team need to be informed about and comfortable with libraries and all the resources they can offer since library services are potential components of any child's IFSP or IEP. Interagency relationships and librarian/parent/professional partnerships provide the mechanisms for sharing information about library service with all the parties involved. Through these partnerships, families become aware of which library services are appropriate and available for their child and these services and programs can be incorporated into the child's individual plans.

Multidisciplinary Evaluation

Children, under Part B or Part C, are entitled to a multidisciplinary evaluation to assess their unique strengths and needs in five areas of development: cognition (learning), speech and language (communication), fine and gross motor (walking and movement), social-emotional (relating to others), and adaptive development (self-help). This evaluation must identify activities and services that build upon the child's strengths to meet his/her identified needs. Only properly trained and licensed individuals are allowed to conduct the evaluation.

The Individualized Family Service Plan (IFSP) under Part C (Children, birth through age three)

As part of this evaluation, the child's family directs an assessment of its own resources, priorities, and concerns to determine ability to meet the developmental needs of the infant or toddler. Once the child is determined eligible, an Individualized Family Service Plan (IFSP) is developed. This service plan

- addresses the child's eligibility, abilities, and areas of need;
- lists the family's resources, priorities for the child, and concerns about the child's development;
- describes the expected goals for the child, how these goals are to be achieved, and time lines to determine the child's progress toward those goals;
- contains a description of what early intervention services are needed and the frequency and duration of those services;
- addresses how these services will be delivered in a natural environment where children without disabilities participate;
- provides specific details regarding the family's expected outcomes for the child and how the evaluation team intends to achieve these outcomes.

Since the family and child's needs change over time, the IFSP is designed to be a fluid document that can be revised at any time by the parent. The parent has the right to choose which service, if any, the child will receive. The IFSP must be reviewed at least once every six months in order to determine if it still best meets the needs of the child and family.

Individualized Education Plan (IEP) under Part B (Preschool-Age Children)

An Individualized Education Plan (IEP), for eligible children under Part B, is developed by a committee designated by the child's school district. This plan serves as the foundation for those providers who are working with the child to improve the areas relative to his/her academic performance. If more than one service is provided to a child, one member of the treating team, usually the child's special education teacher, is designated as the service coordinator. The IEP must be reviewed annually, with the child's progress toward academic goals noted and goals for any future services developed.

Libraries can play a part in developing these plans. The family may request that the evaluation itself or one of the specific services needed by the child take place in a neutral setting or natural environment, one where the child is comfortable. Why not the library? Maybe attendance at the library's storytime could be written into the child's IFSP or IEP to support language and social skills development. Or the library could be used as a community place for screening programs and service delivery. This type of coordination will only occur with a concerted effort on the part of the librarian and an agreement with the early intervention or preschool special education official. Whether the library wants to commit to this extensive a role is an individual decision. Just by making available typical library programs and services as part of the process, however, and focusing on the development of professional skills and knowledge, librarians can join the family and the interdisciplinary team in offering greater options for inclusion and education within communities.

Due Process

Eligible children, whether under Part B or Part C, are entitled to certain legal protections under this law. One of the most important protections involves the family's right to confidentiality. All identifying information about the child and family must be kept confidential by those involved in the early intervention system. In addition, parents have the right to examine all records pertaining to the assessment, screening, eligibility determination of their child and their own IFSP or their child's IEP. They are entitled to written notices, in their native language whenever possible, of any changes in services contained in the IFSP or IEP. Another protection is the timely resolution of complaints by parents. While the dispute is being resolved, the child has the right to continue receiving the services currently being provided.

AMERICANS WITH DISABILITIES ACT (ADA)

The Americans with Disabilities Act (ADA) is a federal law that encourages a proactive approach to serving people with disabilities. It seeks to accomplish this by protecting those with disabilities from discrimination in public access and accommodations, employment, housing, and transportation. All public agencies and private businesses are under obligation to make accommodations to the needs of the disabled unless they can prove that making those accommodations creates a financial hardship or seriously alters the nature of their business.

Although the responsibility to make accommodations for those who are disabled is shared by all employees of any agency, the law requires that any agency that employs more than 50 people must designate a person to assume responsibility for compliance with ADA.

Relative to libraries, the key areas of ADA compliance involve

- assuring nondiscrimination in employment of persons with disabilities;
- assuring equity of access to services and information;
- removing physical and environmental barriers that restrict patrons with disabilities from using the library;
- training staff and the general public in disability awareness issues and the regulations of the law.

Since the law was enacted, most libraries have designated an employee to handle this responsibility, commonly referred to as the ADA coordinator or access librarian. The main responsibilities of this designated person are

- to educate the administration and staff of the library as well as the general public in various aspects of the law;
- to evaluate the environment and services of the library to ensure that they are free of barriers to access for patrons with disabilities;
- to develop and implement services free of barriers for patrons with disabilities;
- to provide information about the services available in a variety of alternate formats (including braille, sign language interpreters, large print, audiotape, and computer discs).

Because many libraries have invested personnel and resources in ensuring equity of employment and access, they are in a good position to make the simple programmatic alterations necessary to include children with disabilities into their regular programs and services. Children's librarians can take responsibility and become key advocates within their own library to make their settings not only accessible but welcoming to families of young children with disabilities. They can

- assess the children's room to ensure that it is wheelchair accessible and identify potential barriers to inclusion and integration;
- develop special collections including braille, large print, talking books, captioned children's videos, adaptive toys, a parents' collection, and materials on disabilities for both children and parents;
- provide assistive technology particularly with computer equipment;
- adapt programs for children with special needs;
- alert patrons through newsletters, flyers, and press releases that the library is willing and able to accommodate children with disabilities;
- contact local agencies and organizations that work with families and young children.

NATIONAL EDUCATION GOALS: AMERICA 2000 ACT

The National Education Goals: America 2000 Act has two tenets that are fundamental to quality library service for children (Brennan, 1992). One goal of this act is to have every child start school ready to learn. Since experts predict that 50 percent of a child's intellectual development occurs before the age of four, it is critical for public libraries to help foster that development by providing activities, services, and materials that facilitate early language acquisition and reading readiness. Early intervention is crucial for children with special needs; the younger the child, the better. Libraries have a real opportunity to reach out and claim service to young children as their domain. Inclusion fosters that mission.

The other fundamental tenet of this law is that every adult American will be literate, possess the knowledge and skills necessary to compete in a global economy, and exercise the rights and responsibilities of citizenship. In many communities across the United States, the public library is the only educational institution available to those who cannot read or write. More and more, libraries are developing innovative ways to reach out to young adults, disabled learners, and people with limited English proficiency, helping them become lifelong learners.

By working with parents at all levels, providing them with information resources, and developing connections with other professionals and organizations serving families, children's librarians have a strong role to play in the implementation of all the laws that promote the greater inclusion of children with disabilities in our communities.

RESOURCES

Brennan, Mary Alice. 1992. *Libraries for the National Education Goals.* Syracuse, N.Y.: *ERIC Digest* 4, no. 1 (June).

Crispen, Joanne L. 1993. *The Americans with Disabilities Act: Its Impact on Libraries/The Library's Responses in "Doable" Steps.* Association of Specialized and Cooperative Library Agencies.

Foos, Donald D. and Nancy C. Pack. 1992. *How Libraries Must Comply with the Americans with Disabilities Act (ADA).* Phoenix, Ariz.: Oryx Press.

Immroth, Barbara Froling and Viki Ash-Geisler, eds. 1995. *Achieving School Readiness.* Chicago: American Library Association.

3 FAMILY-CENTERED PRINCIPLES

The family, as the basic unit of society, bears the responsibility for raising its children. For families who have a child with special needs this responsibility can be daunting. Daily lives are often complicated in the effort to accomplish simple tasks and activities. Yet not only the early years, but also the early months, are crucial to a child's readiness to learn. Interaction with other family members and observation of their activities prepare a child for lifelong openness to learning. The family-centered principles presented in this chapter support and respect the pivotal role of the family in the lives of children and ensure family participation in the provision of services to the child.

Libraries have an opportunity to join with other family-serving organizations in their community in developing and providing family-centered library services. Grounded in a basic respect for individual initiative, quality library service already assumes many of the fundamental tenets and guidelines found in family-centered practice. Libraries are committed to lifelong learning, educational enrichment, and satisfying the informational, cultural, and recreational needs of patrons. Self-initiated learning and respect for diverse cultures go hand-in-hand with family-centered practice.

The underlying principles of the family-centered approach, adopted in 1987 by the Association for the Care of Children's Health with support from the Division of Maternal and Child Health, U.S. Public Health Service, are the bases for the principles in this chapter. They are

- recognition that the family is the constant in the child's life while the service systems and personnel within those systems fluctuate;
- facilitation of parent/professional collaboration;
- sharing of unbiased and complete information with parents about their children on an ongoing basis in an appropriate and supportive manner;
- implementation of appropriate policies and programs that are comprehensive and provide emotional and financial support to meet the needs of families;
- encouragement and facilitation of parent-to-parent support;
- recognition of family strengths and individuality and respect for different methods of coping;
- assurance that the design of comprehensive, coordinated, multidisciplinary service delivery systems is flexible, accessible, and responsive to family-identified needs;

- understanding and incorporating the developmental needs of infants, toddlers, preschoolers, and their families into service delivery systems.

In order to better serve the needs of children with disabilities and their families, librarians need to understand family-centered principles and their relationship to quality library service for all families. Exploring these principles from a library perspective helps to form the development of inclusive policies, programs, and services. This analysis enables librarians to cultivate the library's potential to serve families and children with special needs and foster family-centered communities.

RESPECT THE IMPORTANCE AND INTEGRITY OF THE FAMILY UNIT

Librarians need to recognize that the family is the constant in the child's life and that the family's awareness of the variety of services and resources a library provides is essential to its ability to make use of the library as a community support. To design services that meet the needs of young children, librarians must reach the parent or caregiver and include them.

Working with families is not only in the best interest of the child, but is critical to the stability of public libraries. Strong library support is grounded in regular and consistent use of services, starting at the very earliest age. The most effective way to make library users out of the youngest community members is through family participation. If a family leaves one community, librarians want to ensure that the family will use the local library in the next community. They want all children to become lifelong users and friends. The future of libraries depends on the ongoing support of families.

TREAT PARENTS AS PARTNERS

Building a partnership with the parent is necessary if the librarian is to effectively support the individual development of each child. Parents understand and know their child best. Librarians need to respect this knowledge and build upon the parent/child relationship to encourage family literacy and learning. Inclusion and integration of children with special needs is based upon a strong collaboration between the parent and the librarian. This idea of parent/professional collaboration is not foreign to traditional library practice. Librarians, whether conducting a reference interview or working with children in a program, have a natural tendency to recognize the partnering role required to elicit what it is the patron (child) needs. It is this form of respect and recognition that is required to effectively initiate and sustain the parent/professional partnership.

Library service is enhanced through ongoing communication and procedures and policies that encourage parent participation. Responding to a parent's suggestion about the children's room, request for a particular book or video, or inquiry about a program adaptation for his/her child fosters inclusive services. Developing resources based on a patron's request or need empowers the parent in the partnership process.

PROVIDE UNBIASED AND COMPLETE INFORMATION FOR FAMILIES

When first informed of their child's developmental status, parents of young children with disabilities experience many emotions. Their feelings of love and joy are often overshadowed with disappointment, grief, and anger. After a period of time, parents usually accept the fact that their child faces certain challenges. The first stage in this process often begins with parents questioning their own abilities to parent their child. To ease these doubts, many parents will seek information regarding their child's disability and community resources available to assist their child.

Bailey and Simeonsson documented this need in their article "Assessing the Needs of Families with Handicapped Infants" (Bailey and Simeonsson, 1988, pp. 117–126). They surveyed 34 families using their recently developed Family Needs Survey and found that the most frequently cited parental needs were access to

- information about how to teach their child;
- currently available services;
- services that their child will need in the future;
- reading material about parents who have a child similar to theirs.

Other topics that were of interest to families included information on financial assistance, trained child care providers, explaining their child's disability to others, and assistance in family functioning.

Where do parents find this information? The New York State Developmental Disabilities Council found that parents, especially those of children with special needs, frequently report going to the public library for information soon after being told of their child's special need(s) (Cohen and Simkin, 1994, p. 1). Parents of children with special needs found that public libraries are ideal places to obtain information that is free of bias toward a particular approach or service. It is important to note that this need for information by parents of children with disabilities is ongoing, comparable to the needs of most parents when faced with a new developmental stage of their child (D'Amato and Yoshida, 1991, pp. 246–254).

Helping parents locate information is central to the library's basic mission. Providing access to resources for parents and adults who work with children enhances the role of the children's librarian and provides the community support all families need in raising children. Families who have children with disabilities are particularly in need of information regarding the disability, how to advocate for their child to receive services, and the management of the day-to-day tasks of caring for their child.

How the librarian provides service to parents is critical. Developing active listening and communication skills is a must. Housing the parents collection in the children's room reduces barriers and makes it convenient for parents to approach with questions and concerns. Providing information in a variety of formats, covering all aspects and sides of an issue in a nonjudgmental, unbiased way, is particularly important for parents who need to make decisions regarding their child's special needs. Librarians are especially attuned to this need for neutrality.

DEVELOP PROGRAMS, POLICIES, AND SERVICES TO FACILITATE FAMILY LITERACY AND LEARNING

Babies, toddlers, preschoolers, and early elementary age children do not visit the library independently. They must be accompanied by an adult, usually a parent or caregiver. Legally, the children's librarian is never *in loco parentis*. This presents a wonderful opportunity for librarians to serve children within the family unit, focusing on the child's as well as the parent's or caregiver's needs. Services should reflect a family approach, recognizing that the parent's comfort with the library will be reflected in the child's comfort level.

Programs need to be designed with that dyad in mind. In storytime or a Parent/Child Workshop, librarians need to focus on the parent and child learning together and support the parent-as-teacher role. The librarian serves as a facilitator of family learning, encouraging the parent to become involved in the child's earliest learning activities.

FACILITATE PARENT-TO-PARENT SUPPORT

Building community, though not a traditional role of the public library, could be a complementary role for children's services. Incorporating parent services within the children's department allows the librarian the opportunity to assist in developing networks among parents. The library itself provides a common meeting ground for children and families. It is a place to meet other parents and engage in social exchange. A library's Parent/Child Workshop or storytime often stimulates the formation of local play groups or the initiation of new friendships. Assisting in the development of baby-sitting cooperatives, playgroups, parent support groups, or parent-to-parent networks, especially for parents of children who have special needs, is a natural extension of traditional children's services.

BUILD ON FAMILY STRENGTHS AND RECOGNIZE CULTURAL DIVERSITY

The library's mission is to serve the entire community, respecting and celebrating the diversity it represents. Libraries pride themselves on being democratic institutions, encouraging use of the library by all individuals. This fundamental characteristic of public library service dovetails with family-centered principles, particularly as librarians work with families that exhibit a variety of special needs. As is true of all library patrons, the child with a disability and the family are recognized for their individual needs and differences and appropriate service is provided accordingly. It is important to keep library service to families and children free at the point of entry. This tradition of public library service, where no one is denied access to the library's resources, fosters inclusion.

ESTABLISH LINKAGES WITH COMMUNITY SERVICES THAT SERVE FAMILIES AND CHILDREN

By listening and establishing relationships with families, the librarian is in a position to help parents find the local resources they need for themselves and their children. This information is not always easily available. Librarians need to build coalitions and networks with the larger community of family service providers and learn about what other services are available for families. It is only through this coordinated effort that librarians can give families information they need, when they need it.

The librarian can be not only a key link between families and the resources that the professional community provides, but a critical partner in providing coordination and continuity for family support professionals. The librarian's skills in collection development and organization, accessing resources, and providing reference service enhance community networks. The library can serve as a central place for storing materials, sharing information, and providing meeting space.

DESIGN DEVELOPMENTALLY APPROPRIATE SERVICES

When designing services to meet the needs of young children, librarians need to integrate the developmental needs of infants, toddlers, and preschoolers into the library environment. Adaptations for children with special needs can only be successful when the librarian understands the basic concepts of developmental appropriateness for all children.

DEVELOPMENTALLY APPROPRIATE PRACTICE

Developmentally appropriate practice applies our knowledge of child development to making decisions about how we provide library service to young children. It is not a set of rigid rules and procedures but a framework or philosophy of service that means providing services that are child-centered, based on data and information about what children are like at different stages of development. It is a basic respect for a child's developmental needs and cultural background.

When looking at services within a developmentally appropriate framework, librarians need to look at developmental milestones, the relationship of the child to the parent/caregiver, the child's understanding of his environment and surroundings, and the interplay of library resources within the context of the child's experiences. Basic principles of child development that all professionals who work with children need to understand include (Gestwicki, 1995, pp. 8–9):

1. There is a predictable sequence in development.
2. Development at one stage lays the base for later development.
3. There are optimal periods in development.
4. Development results from the interaction of biological factors (maturation) and environmental factors (learning).
5. Development proceeds as an interrelated whole, with all aspects (physical, cognitive, emotional, social) influencing the others.
6. Each individual develops according to a particular timetable and pace.
7. Development proceeds from simple to complex, and from general to specific.

It must be remembered that nothing is clear cut or absolute when applying these principles to practice. Librarians need to examine their programs and practices based on the whole environment and determine whether they enhance or diminish the quality of the child's (and family's) experience within the library.

Children with disabilities develop continuously too. New research indicates that all children have multiple intelligences, that is, ways of knowing. Most people can appreciate skills in language and mathematics as signs of ability and intelligence. Far less understood is the idea that children have other ways of knowing, namely: bodily-kinesthetic, spatial, musical, interpersonal and intra-personal intelligences. Helping a child with a disability tap into alternative ways of knowing, rather than depending upon a sense or body part that may not be functioning, is a major focus of intervention and education (Burchfield, 1996, pp. 4–8). Recognizing the importance of this approach is one way that librarians can enhance the lives of children with disabilities. By being aware of their individual needs and strengths, appreciating their various ways of knowing, and making appropriate adaptations, librarians are providing access to library service in the most optimal sense.

DEVELOPMENTAL MILESTONES

Although every child develops differently and according to his/her own timetable, the vantage point of the librarian, who has many experiences with young children and families, does open up the possibility of the librarian noticing "something different about a particular child" or parents asking the librarian questions regarding their children's development. Although not in a position to give advice, it is appropriate for the librarian to understand the basic developmental milestones and to assist parents if there are concerns, referring them to appropriate services when necessary.

Being familiar with developmental milestones is important for librarians when they are designing programs for young children. Appendix B provides a quick checklist of developmental milestones for children, birth through five years of age. This list of milestones will assist librarians in designing age-appropriate activities. Other guidelines to keep in mind:

> Young children, with and without disabilities, should be engaged in activities that allow them to become aware of, explore, inquire about, and utilize new concepts, skills, and materials. Any activity or material should be meaningful, engaging, and relevant to the child.
>
> No activity should require a very young child to separate from the parent or caregiver.
>
> Activities need to consider the parent/child dyad as the most critical factor when designing library-based early childhood programs.
>
> Each child should be allowed to move at his or her own pace in skill acquisition.
>
> The process, not the product, is what matters in young children's learning.

Using these basic guidelines, librarians can assess the programs they are currently offering as well as initiate new services or programs. By meshing basic library service with developmentally and educationally appropriate practice and family-centered principles, librarians will maximize the learning process and enhance the effectiveness of a young child's experience within the library setting.

RESOURCES FOR DESIGNING DEVELOPMENTALLY APPROPRIATE SERVICES

Association for Library Service to Children. 1996. *Programming for Young Children: Birth through Age Five*. Chicago: American Library Association.

Bredekamp, Sue. 1987. *Developmentally Appropriate Practice in Early Childhood Programs Serving Children from Birth through Age Eight*. Washington, D.C.: National Association for Education of Young Children. (periodically updated)

Brickman, Nancy Altman and Lynn Spencer Taylor. 1991. *Supporting Young Learners: Ideas for Preschool and Day Care Providers*. Ypsilanti, Mich.: High/Scope Press.

Carlson, Ann D. 1985. *Early Childhood Literature Sharing Programs in Libraries*. Hamden, Conn.: Library Professional Publications.

Feinberg, Sandra and Kathleen Deerr. 1995. *Running a Parent/Child Workshop: A How-To-Do-It Manual for Librarians*. New York: Neal-Schuman.

Feinberg, Sandra and Sari Feldman. 1996. *Serving Families and Children through Partnerships: A How-To-Do-It Manual for Librarians*. New York: Neal-Schuman.

Feinberg, Sandra, Joan Kuchner, and Sari Feldman. 1998. *Learning Environments for Young Children: Rethinking Library Spaces and Services*. Chicago: ALA Editions.

Gestwicki, Carol. 1995. *Developmentally Appropriate Practice: Curriculum and Development in Early Education*. Albany, N.Y.: Delmar.

Giacomo, Pete and Marilyn Getts. 1985. "Children's Services in a Developmental Key." *Top of the News* (Spring): 267–273.

Greene, Ellin. 1991. *Books, Babies, and Libraries: Serving Infants, Toddlers, Their Parents, and Caregivers*. Chicago: American Library Association.

Hohmann, Mary, Bernard Banet, and David P. Weikart. 1979. *Young Children in Action: A Manual for Preschool Educators*. Ypsilanti, Mich.: High/Scope Press.

Marino, Jane. 1992. *Mother Goose Time: Library Programs for Babies and Their Caregivers*. Bronx, N.Y.: H.W. Wilson.

Mitchell, Anne and Judy David, eds. 1992. *Explorations with Young Children: A Curriculum Guide from Bank Street College of Education*. Mt. Rainier, Md.: Gryphon House.

Nespeca, Sue McCleaf. 1994. *Library Programming for Families with Young Children: A How-To-Do-It Manual For Librarians*. New York: Neal-Schuman.

Neuman, Susan B. and Kathy Roskos. 1990. "Play, Print, and Purpose: Enriching Play Environments for Literacy Development." *The Reading Teacher* 44, no. 3 (November): 214–221.

REFERENCES

Bailey, D. and R. Simeonsson. 1988. "Assessing the Needs of Families with Handicapped Infants." *Journal of Special Education* 2, no. 1:117–126.

Burchfield, David. 1996. "Teaching ALL Children: Four Developmentally Appropriate Curricular and Instructional Strategies in Primary Grade Classrooms." *Young Children* (November): 4–8.

Cohen B. P. and L. S. Simkin. 1994. *Library Based Parent Resource Centers: A Guide to Implementing Programs*. Albany, N.Y.: New York State Developmental Disabilities Planning Council and New York Library Association.

D'Amato, Ellen and Roland K. Yoshida. 1991. "Parental Needs: An Educational Life Cycle Perspective." *Journal of Early Intervention* 15, no. 3: 246–254.

Gestwicki, Carol. 1995. *Developmentally Appropriate Practice: Curriculum and Development in Early Education.* Albany, N.Y.: Delmar.

4 RESOURCE-BASED PRACTICE

How do individuals react when they encounter a serious personal problem? To whom do they turn for support? A significant other or best friend? Their immediate family? Their minister, rabbi, or priest, co-workers, bowling partners, or neighbors? Chances are that they would seek support and help from one of these trusted and familiar "community" members before going to a mental health or medical professional. Families of children with disabilities feel similarly. Unfortunately, families of children with disabilities often do not receive the support they need from these informal community sources. Why not?

WHY COMMUNITY SUPPORT IS LACKING

When families of children with disabilities do not receive community support it is not because it is impossible to provide this support. The two main reasons that such support is not forthcoming are that the community has become accustomed to leaving the care of children with disabilities to institutions or other professionals and, furthermore, community members simply are not used to interacting with these children and are anxious about their own behavior; however, these conditions need not persist.

RELIANCE ON PROFESSIONAL HELP

Traditionally, children with disabilities have been either institutionalized or cared for by multiple professionals. This has often led to isolation and a lack of connection to the informal support networks that exist within all communities.

Although these families need the technical and therapeutic advice and support of specialists with expert advice on how to position a child, elicit language, develop cognitive skills, and facilitate gross motor development, being an "expert" does not necessarily mean that a professional is supportive. Just like any other family, families of children with disabilities sometimes need a good listener, another parent who is willing to share practical ideas, or a friendly neighbor who will invite a child to a birthday party. An informal community support network, so necessary to a family's sense of being included, may not fit easily into lives filled with a complex web of appointments, therapies, and treatments.

NEED TO EDUCATE PUBLIC

In some instances, community members shy away from giving help and support out of an anxiety of not knowing what to do or how to behave toward the child with a disability. Though antidiscrimination laws have broken through legal barriers, social situations are often difficult and awkward for those individuals who have had few encounters with handicapping conditions.

More and more children with significant disabilities are surviving birth due to medical and technological advances. Community members, unaccustomed to seeing children with oxygen machines, tracheotomies, or communication devices, are uncomfortable and fearful of what is unfamiliar.

Fear frequently leads to stereotypes about children with disabilities and ignorance about the disabilities themselves. Children who are physically challenged are often assumed to have mental disabilities as well; people talk loudly to the vision impaired and view a child in a wheelchair as someone who will never live an independent life. Stereotypes and ignorance about disabling conditions can usually be eliminated through experience, open communication, increased contact, and a broader knowledge base.

By integrating inclusive practices, the library can be an effective agent in reducing fear and prejudice toward children with disabilities. It can create a comfortable environment for families to get together. Familiarity leads to comfort and trust. Trust is necessary to build friendship and support.

WHAT IS RESOURCE-BASED PRACTICE?

When parents discover that their child has a disability, the family is often thrust into a complex, service-based system. The child accesses professionally delivered services at a special school or clinic that isolates him/her from typically developing peers and the network of informal community supports. This system is expensive to maintain in an era of shrinking dollars.

A new approach to service delivery, known as "resource-based practice," focuses on the identification and utilization of *all* resources within the community. In this model, a resource is defined as "the full range of possible types of community help or assistance—potentially useful information, experiences, opportunities, etc.—that might be mobilized and used to meet the needs of an individual or group. Resources are a means to accomplishing a desired outcome including, but not limited to, different kinds of community learning opportunities for enhancing and promoting child and family competence" (Trivette, Dunst, and Deal, 1996, p.7). This approach to providing services is an opportunity for libraries.

Consider that all children and families belong to multiple communities. These communities—which include extended families, neighborhoods, churches, workplaces, child care settings, libraries, sports leagues, scouting organizations, and other resources—have the potential to provide support. The goal of resource-based practice is to increase utilization of these community resources, rather than just professionally provided services, as a way to enhance and support child, parent, and family functioning. Research has demonstrated that parents of children with disabilities, exposed to a resource-based approach, feel that their children achieve greater gains and that they themselves have more control over service provision (Trivette, Dunst, and Deal, 1996, p. 15).

HOW THE LIBRARY "FITS IN"

A public library is one of the community's greatest assets. Librarians can provide families with a valuable source of information and support by using their information retrieval, technological, programmatic, and referral skills. For families of children with special needs, this support is not dependent upon the child meeting eligibility criteria, often deficit based or income limited. The library's capacity to provide access to information, an array of programs and resources for young children, and a child-centered community environment make it particularly applicable within this resource-based model.

THE LIBRARY AS A COMMUNITY "PLACE"

Many libraries offer services that can serve as informal supports for families of children with disabilities. Parents have access to valuable information and an opportunity to gain emotional and social support from their peers. Library-based infant/toddler and preschool programs offer the young child with a disability the chance to learn from and play with children who are developing typically. Many libraries have created mini-environments with toys and learning materials that are aimed at young children. These areas are welcoming to young children and can be especially helpful for families looking for a "natural" community environment in which to interact with other children and their families.

As a community place, the library also provides a variety of opportunities for service providers. Proactive marketing encourages providers of early intervention and special education preschool services to make use of the library's resources. The following strategies are just a few of the many ways in which providers can utilize the library to integrate children with disabilities within the community. Providers can

1. Use the library as an alternative site for the provision of services.
2. Bring a child with a disability to a library program.
3. Assist in designing an adaptation within the library setting.
4. Visit the library with the family and help them access the resources.
5. Serve as a resource to the library staff so they can more effectively serve children with disabilities and their families.

THE LIBRARIAN AS A COMMUNITY RESOURCE PERSON

Resource-based practice provides librarians with a wonderful opportunity to exhibit their professional skills. Traditional library roles are exactly what is needed for providing community services: information and referral specialist, program adapter and developer, special collections developer, coalition builder and networker, and educator and advocate for parenting services.

Information and Referral Specialist

One of the key elements of the resource-based approach is the identification of community services, a natural fit for the information role of the public librarian. Skilled at locating resources within communities through access to collections, community databases, vertical files, interlibrary loan, and the Internet, librarians can empower parents to use all of the community's resources and not just professionally based services.

As the survival of children with significant disabilities increases, more parents are in need of often hard-to-locate information and resources. A family of a child with a disability may need resources in the areas of medicine, early intervention and preschool special services, public and private education, entitlement programs, assistive technology, inclusionary child care situations, sibling support, insurance, custom vehicles, permanency planning, living wills, trust funds, and advocacy training. Identifying these resources may fall at the bottom of a long list of caregiving chores for parents. As a family support professional, librarians can assist parents by helping them locate much-needed sources of information and assistance.

Identifying these supports will not be a once-only task. Since the library is one of the most stable organizations within the community, librarians should anticipate that the family will probably turn to them for support throughout the child's entire life cycle. The librarian's role as information and referral specialist will be called upon repeatedly by parents as their child ages and new experiences require different information and adaptations. The value of this kind of support cannot be overemphasized, and it is often this support that fortifies parents to carry on their important role as caregiver.

A good illustration of the tremendous impact a library can have can be found in the story of Danny. A three-year-old boy with cerebral palsy, Danny first came into the library with his mother and siblings to participate in *Special Time*, a program for young children with disabilities and their families. His only means of mobility was his stroller or his mother carrying him and, then, holding him in a sitting or standing position when he wanted to play. Through the resource people, introduced during the course of the program, and other resources identified by the librarian, his mother learned about getting a wheelchair fitted to his size and needs. She found out about how to access the financial supports necessary to purchase the wheelchair. With the wheelchair, Danny was able to participate in many more activities without his mother having to physically support his body. As he grew older, his family called upon these same resources to obtain a motorized wheelchair, increasing his self-sufficiency and independence.

In time, both he and the wheelchair got too heavy for his family to lift in and out of the car. His mother again sought information on how she might obtain a van with a hydraulic lift. In addition to the grant opportunities and other resources, the librarian mentioned the possibility of approaching local service groups such as the Rotary and Kiwanis Clubs for assistance. She located their addresses and the names of their officers. A few weeks later this same librarian was making a presentation at a meeting of the Rotary Club. Before her talk, the club president was reviewing the correspondence for that month, which included a letter from Danny's family. During her presentation, which just happened to include slides of Danny and other children who had participated in the *Special Time* program, the librarian was able to introduce him to the group. She talked about his progress and potential and matched a face and a family's story with the request for assistance. That afternoon the club voted to provide monetary support toward the purchase of a van with a hydraulic lift. Danny's story exemplifies how the librarian as an information specialist and advocate can support children with disabilities and their families.

Program Adapter and Developer

Including families and children with disabilities in library service may require adaptations of programs. Successful adaptations, often simple to implement, require planning and collaboration with parents and other family support agencies. These plans must respect and incorporate the needs of library patrons who are not disabled while encouraging the inclusion of families and children with disabilities. Librarians, who already appreciate the complexities involved in delivering programs to the community at large, must take the lead in adapting programs to meet the needs of families and young children with disabilities. Chapter 8 offers general guidelines to help librarians to implement simple adaptations within typical library-based programs for young children.

Special Collections Developer

To better serve families of children with special needs, librarians may want to consider developing special collections. Parent resource centers, adaptive toy lending collections, pamphlet files, information kits for parents, electronic resources, and assistive technology are just some of the possibilities. Chapters 9 through 12 provide specific guidelines on how to develop special collections for this audience.

Coalition Builder and Networker

Building coalitions among agencies and organizations is a critical role for librarians and key to impacting the lives of library patrons with young children. In *Serving Families and Children through Partnerships* (Feinberg and Feldman, 1996, pp. 13–14), the authors emphasize that "through the development of coalitions and networks, librarians can expand their horizons, become more-informed professionals, and be alerted to trends in youth services, early childhood, and parent education. They can integrate the library's youth and parenting services with the greater community of services and increase the library's potential for reaching families. In addition to what the librarian will gain, parents and professionals will learn

- to recognize the library's ability to organize and disseminate information to its community;
- to understand the role of the library in providing free access to information;
- to look toward the library as a primary community center for serving families and young children;
- to place the library and the children's librarian in a leadership role in advocating for youth and family services;
- to appreciate the library's role in sharing community resources, building a democratic nation and beginning the lifelong learning process."

Building coalitions and partnerships is essential for librarians who wish to effectively implement inclusionary practices within their libraries.

Chapter 7 discusses the competencies needed to develop collaborative services, including a list of resources to improve networking skills.

Educator and Advocate for Parenting Services

To effectively serve children with special needs, librarians need to work closely with parents. Working in partnership with parents requires that librarians take a broader view of the role of the children's services librarian. No young child comes to the library unless attended by a parent/caregiver. It is the children's librarian's job to advocate for service to parents within the library setting, emphasizing that literacy begins at birth and that parents are the child's first and most important teachers. Chapter 6 provides strategies and techniques to assist librarians in their work with parents.

Resource-based practice has opened up a window of opportunity for libraries and librarians. Establishing the library as a main player in providing services and a natural environment for young children, including those with special needs, and their parents will ensure long-term survival for libraries as community centers that are truly responsive to the needs of all segments of their communities.

REFERENCES

Feinberg, Sandra and Sari Feldman. 1996. *Serving Children and Families through Partnerships*. New York: Neal-Schuman.

Trivette, Carol M., Carl J. Dunst, and Angela G. Deal. 1996. "Resource-Based Early Intervention Practices." In *The Contexts of Early Intervention: Systems and Settings* by S. K. Thurman et al. Baltimore: Paul H. Brookes.

PART II:
GETTING YOUR
LIBRARY READY

5 ASSESSING AND TRAINING YOUR STAFF

Assessing staff attitudes and competencies, understanding the characteristics and needs of families of children with disabilities as a patron group, and training staff are some of the initial steps to consider before embarking on service development. *Accessibility*—physical accessibility, collections and programs accessibility, and attitudinal accessibility—is the essential goal for inclusionary practices when examining library readiness. Staff generally understand that modifying the physical environment to accommodate wheelchairs, adapting a program to include a child with a disability, or adding assistive technology to a computer station makes libraries more accessible. What they may have difficulty understanding is that staff attitudes and competencies are most important and set the framework for an inclusive library.

Individuals with disabilities often cite insufficient staff training, awareness, and sensitivity, rather than costly architectural modifications or expensive equipment and services, as key issues when addressing barriers to inclusion. A library can have the best written policies, adaptive technologies, resources, and collections, but unless the staff has a genuine understanding of and commitment to inclusion, children with disabilities and their families will not feel welcomed. Achieving this level of understanding and commitment is a process that involves the reexamination of attitudes, comfort levels, expectations, and skills of all library employees, not just those providing direct service to children.

STAFF ATTITUDE ASSESSMENT

Traditionally, children's staff strive to provide a nonthreatening, nonjudgmental atmosphere within the library, offering a wide range of services specially designed for young children. A child's smiling, inquisitive face is like a magnet that brings out the librarian's best qualities—warm, solicitous, nurturing. For many children's librarians, the early childhood years are the most endearing and rewarding.

INITIAL REACTIONS

When a child has a disability, however, the initial response may not be so positive. While most library staff in theory support the concept of including children with special needs, when faced with reality, they often have mixed feelings. Each library employee brings his or her own life experiences, skills, and comfort levels to the workplace. For inclusion to work, librarians need to acknowledge personal attitudes, feelings, and experiences and the reactions they may engender in response to children with disabling conditions and their families. Library readiness for inclusion begins with honest personal assessment.

Different disabilities often generate different responses. Working with children who have a *physical* disability is probably the least anxiety provoking for staff. They recognize immediately that a disability exists. The presence of physical clues helps the librarian and other staff assess the situation and anticipate what adaptations may be necessary to meet the patron's needs. When a library has sufficient resources and the librarian can anticipate some of the necessary adaptations required for helping the individual, comfort level is high. For example, if a young child is blind, the librarian may suggest talking, braille, or tactile books, or introduce the child to a listening station. The parent may be directed to a variety of books and local resources that focus on parenting a child who is visually impaired.

A child whose disability is accompanied by a severe disfigurement may present a different reaction. Staff may be reluctant to look at the child lest they be accused of "staring." They may avoid the family altogether or deal only with the parent, not acknowledging the child. In some instances, staff may be overly sympathetic or present an over-protective attitude. This can limit the child's natural participation in the library environment and can make communication with the parent awkward and strained.

With a child who has an apparent *mental* or *emotional* disability, expectations for behavior and cognitive ability are often ambivalent. If speech is loud and/or difficult to understand and behavior viewed as disturbing to other children, the librarian may feel uncertain about how to approach the parent and determine the needs of the child and family. There may be a tendency to interact only with the parent, avoiding direct contact with the child, or make the interaction as brief as possible, sending the family on its way before anything "unpleasant" happens. In these situations, the staff's feelings of inadequacy, helplessness, and lack of control will often be conveyed and are not conducive to promoting inclusion.

When the staff is aware that a physical or mental disability exists, their frustration generally results from personal feelings of inadequacy rather than attributing blame to the child or parents. This is not the case with the "hidden" disability. If children show no physical or other obvious differences, it is assumed they are developing typically. When children behave inappropriately, in a manner other than would normally be anticipated for their age, they and their parents may be judged and blamed. Staff may feel angry, resentful, and apprehensive about having the child visit the library.

Acknowledging that some type of disability may be precipitating this behavior is the first step toward a more successful experience for this child in the library. Staff need to focus on the individual child's strengths and move beyond their initial emotional reactions. Skill development in meeting the challenges that inappropriate behavior presents in the library setting can come through heightened awareness and increased training and experience. To make the child's library experience rich and successful, and to help the staff feel adequate to the task, specific techniques and methods for coping with a range of behaviors need to be acquired.

Changing perceptions and attitudes, though never easy, is best initiated through a personal assessment. Before a change in attitude can occur, the staff needs to honestly assess their individual attitudes regarding disabilities and the library's role in the inclusion process. The Personal Attitude Checklist (Figure 5–1) and the corresponding Response to Staff Issues and Concerns section of this chapter can serve as catalysts for the exploration of feelings and attitudes and guide staff to an understanding and awareness of their own biases.

Figure 5–1. Personal Attitude Checklist

ATTITUDE CHECKLIST

	AGREE	DISAGREE
1. Other professionals, agencies, and organizations are already in place to serve young children with disabilities and their families. The library should not compete with them.	___	___
2. Young children with disabilities cannot attend regular library programs because they are receiving services in an agency-based program during regular hours.	___	___
3. I am a librarian, not an early intervention or preschool special education professional. If I wanted to work with children with disabilities, I would have become a special education teacher.	___	___
4. It is a librarian's job to obtain a basic knowledge of the various disabilities they may encounter so they can support individual children and their parents in the library setting.	___	___
5. It is the parent's responsibility to control the behavior of their children while in the library. It is not the librarian's job to intervene.	___	___
6. Serving young children with special needs consumes a disproportionate amount of resources and takes away from the majority of children needing the library.	___	___
7. Parents of typically developing children feel uncomfortable in an inclusive setting and may stop coming to the library.	___	___
8. Children with certain behavioral and control issues may pose a danger to other children.	___	___
9. Parents don't want their children to learn inappropriate behaviors that some children with special needs may exhibit.	___	___
10. The library is in a unique position to offer opportunities for young children with disabilities and their families.	___	___
11. Librarians are not trained and feel inadequate when working with families and children with disabilities.	___	___

RESPONSE TO STAFF ISSUES AND CONCERNS

Examining individual feelings and attitudes regarding young children with disabilities and their families is a critical first step toward building inclusive practices. Use the Personal Attitude Checklist (page 42) as a tool to begin this process. Discuss staff concerns and issues together, referring to the section on Response to Staff Issues and Concerns. These discussions often lead to the breakdown of barriers and increased sensitivity and awareness among staff. The following suggestions will help you encourage your staff to be open to inclusive practices.

Attitude: Other professionals, agencies, and organizations are already in place to serve young children with disabilities and their families. The library should not attempt to compete with them.

Response: Early intervention and preschool special education programs do not provide early childhood library services. Nor do they necessarily provide the natural or least restrictive environment that is required by federal and state laws. Early intervention staff and the families they serve need access to community-based resources. In addition to day care centers and nursery schools, library-based early childhood services help fill this need. Such service is not competing with but rather supplementing and enhancing early intervention services, providing an opportunity for lifelong learning and skills development using the local library.

Attitude: Young children with disabilities cannot attend regular library programs because they are receiving services in an agency-based program during regular hours.

Response: Today, more and more young children with disabilities are receiving their early intervention or preschool special education services in the natural setting of their homes. This type of service delivery allows for greater flexibility in a family's ability and motivation to attend library programs. Parents and providers often schedule special services around or within the child's community activities such as swim programs, storytimes, or playgroups.

There are many children who are unable to attend library programs due to full-time enrollment in day care or preschool programs. Recognizing this trend, librarians may need to consider outreach services, providing on-site programs or training for center staff. Weekend, evening, and vacation programs, designed specially for young children who cannot attend weekday programs, is another alternative for librarians to consider, not just for children with special needs but for all families with busy schedules.

Attitude: I am a librarian, not an early intervention specialist. If I had wanted to work with children with disabilities, I would have become a special education teacher.

Response: If libraries are to remain vital, significant institutions within their communities, it is essential that they anticipate and respond to the needs and changes in society. The role of the library and the children's librarian is constantly evolving. The seventies brought an array of audiovisual collections and services. The eighties saw the lowering of the age requirements for children's programming and a recognition of our role in service to adults who live and/or work with children. The nineties bring ever-changing technology and the greater inclusion of individuals with disabilities. Two decades ago, library service to children traditionally began at three years of age. Now it begins at birth and includes service for parents and professionals who work with families. In the beginning of each of these changes, the expansion beyond traditional services and client groups was uncomfortable for many librarians. Today these services and audiences are considered standard fare for public libraries.

This evolution is now in process regarding library service to children with special needs. Their participation in the full range of library programs and routines is new and untested. Librarians who work with babies, toddlers, and community agencies feel no role confusion with nannies, child care providers, or community social workers. As library professionals, their role is clearly to provide library service to *all* of the children and families within their community. To include children with special needs, they need to adapt their methods so that these children can make full use of the library's resources.

Attitude: I can't become an expert on every behavioral and developmental disability.

Response: It is a librarian's job to obtain a basic knowledge of the various clientele they may encounter in the library so that they can provide quality community service. Supporting individual children and their families in a library setting is the job of every children's librarian. Knowledge of any client group is essential to plan appropriate library service for that group. Knowledge, however, does not imply in-depth knowledge or expertise. Few children's librarians are experts in every aspect of early childhood development, but they do have enough knowledge to deliver library service in a developmentally appropriate manner. Acquiring general knowledge about children with disabilities is part of this process.

To start educating your staff about your clients' needs, assess the make-up of the library's population. The school district or public health department may be able to provide statistics on how many children residing in the library's service area have disabling conditions. Obtain further information on serving children with particular disabilities by speaking with parents, contacting early intervention or preschool special education providers working in the community, and consulting resources within the library itself.

Attitude: It is the parent's responsibility to control the behavior of their children while in the library. It is not the librarian's job to intervene.

Response: Legally, library staff is not *in loco parentis*. And while it is not their job to intervene in a manner that oversteps parental authority, librarians often experience two emotions when children are disruptive. First, their common sense dictates the need to provide a setting that protects all children's right to a safe and pleasant experience. Second, they want to support parents whenever possible. Because of these feelings, most librarians are motivated to become involved.

No one would argue that staff members should intervene if they see a young child doing something that would result in possible injury to himself or another child. Staff members routinely assist parents by opening doors for strollers and heading off darting toddlers before they get into unsafe situations. By talking and working together with parents, librarians and staff can be an integral part of a strategy that supports the authority of the parent. Modeling good communication techniques for parents by conveying expectations in a clear and consistent manner helps the child understand appropriate library behavior and allows families to feel comfortable in the library setting. Chapter 6 focuses on specific communication strategies with parents.

Attitude: Serving young children with special needs consumes a disproportionate amount of resources and takes away from the majority of children needing the library.

Response: Whenever a library expands services to a particular group, some may feel it is taking resources away from those already served. It was not different when libraries first began to serve children and share resources with adult services. Good customer service encourages target marketing, reaching out to new audiences, and refining services based on patron needs. Young children with disabilities are patrons with the same right to library service as other young children. The Americans with Disabilities Act is in place to ensure this, mandating the provision of "reasonable accommodations" to all persons with disabilities. Inclusion of children with disabilities broadens the range of service and fulfills the library's mission as a public institution.

Attitude: Parents of typically developing children feel uncomfortable in an inclusive setting and may stop coming to the library.

Response: People fear what they do not know. Educating the community on the benefits of inclusion for all children and families and providing opportunities for families to voice their concerns will go a long way in preparing families for an inclusive experience. The best method to alleviate anxious feelings and fears is to have families with typically developing children participate in inclusive settings. Observing the acceptance that their own children exhibit toward children with disabilities diminishes discomfort and often engenders a sense of pride.

Attitude: Children with certain behavior control issues sometimes pose a danger to other children.

Response: Behavior problems are present when serving all young children. Who hasn't experienced an occasional biting toddler or a frustrated preschooler ready to hurl some blocks? A toddler with a temper tantrum can wreak havoc in storytime and test the skills of even the most experienced librarian. Two basic rules help to prevent these problems. Materials and activities need to be developmentally appropriate and the room or program must be adequately staffed. Problems occur much less frequently when there is a range of materials and appropriate staff-to-child ratio.

Library staff must learn to read behaviors and subtle signs that are precursors to rough physical behavior and be ready to intervene and redirect the child. It is important that library staff be trained and feel comfortable when intervening to ensure that all library patrons feel safe.

Attitude: Parents don't want their children to learn inappropriate behaviors that some children with special needs may exhibit.

Response: There is no evidence to suggest that typically developing children regress or learn inappropriate behaviors from their peers with disabilities. In actuality, children often become more sensitive or protective. The more opportunities children have to interact with children of different ages, cultures, and abilities, the more accepting and understanding they will become and the more aware they will be of similarities rather than differences.

Attitude: Librarians are not trained and feel inadequate when working with families and children with disabilities.

Response: Inclusion not only requires the development of new skills, but learning how to apply existing skills to new situations. Some type of initial as well as ongoing training may be necessary. Reading this book and discussing it with peers provides a first step in the determination of training needs. The next step is to examine the competencies needed for inclusion.

The library is in a unique position to offer opportunities for young children with disabilities and their families. Few community-based institutions offer as many positive and supportive opportunities for children with special needs as libraries. Other public and private institutions have requirements for fees, skills, age limits, membership or other eligibility criteria that can actually exclude rather than include these children. Because many libraries have modified their buildings for handicapped accessibility and made a commitment to the Americans with Disabilities Act, policies and practices to remove barriers are often in place. Many librarians have been trained in listening skills, customer service, and information and referral techniques.

By including children with disabilities in the library setting and supporting their families with information and referral services, materials, and resources, libraries have the opportunity to give these families not only access to resources, but a sense of belonging. A secure base empowers families to seek additional means of informal support—such as friends or child care providers—and to learn about government and private agencies, advocacy groups, and community networks.

COMPETENCIES

The introduction to *Competencies for Librarians Serving Children in Public Libraries* (Association for Library Service to Children, 1989) states that "librarians must be alert to the changes in society which necessitate changes in library service and the acquisition of additional competencies. Thus it is understood that professional growth and development is a lifelong process." No employee's job is static. It evolves and grows in response to community and library needs. To implement inclusive practices, it is critical for all levels of library staff, from a page to a coordinator of children's services, to gain new skills. Using these competencies, which are adapted from the Association for Library Service to Children's publication, librarians can examine their own skills and behaviors relative to serving families of children with special needs.

ADMINISTRATION AND MANAGEMENT SKILLS
- Participates in all aspects of the library's planning process in order to articulate the needs of children with disabilities.
- Includes the needs of children with disabilities when setting long- and short-range goals, objectives, and priorities.
- Analyzes the costs of library services to families and children with special needs in order to develop, justify, and evaluate a budget.

- Identifies training resources within the community and implements training opportunities for all levels of staff working with families.
- Demonstrates problem-solving, decision-making, and mediation techniques to implement inclusion.
- Identifies outside sources of funding and writes effective grant applications to help fund inclusive services.

COMMUNICATION SKILLS

- Defines and communicates the needs of children with disabilities and their families so that administrators, library staff, and members of the larger community understand how inclusion fits into basic children's services.
- Demonstrates sensitivity and interpersonal skills when meeting with children, parents, and early intervention and preschool special education providers.
- Applies active listening skills.
- Conveys a nonjudgmental attitude toward patrons and their requests.

MATERIALS AND COLLECTION DEVELOPMENT

- Demonstrates a knowledge of materials in all formats for young children, including those with various disabilities, as well as materials for parents and professionals.
- Keeps abreast of new materials that broaden access for children with disabilities.
- Develops appropriate collections and knows how and where to access additional materials.
- Provides access to adaptive materials or demonstrates creativity in adapting readily available materials to meet the needs of children with disabilities.
- Educates users on technology and software developed for children with disabilities, including Internet resources.

PROGRAMMATIC SKILLS

- Designs, promotes, adapts, executes, and evaluates programs for young children, based on their developmental needs and interests.
- Presents a variety of performers and programs and provides accessibility to such programs for all children.
- Establishes programs and services for parents, individuals, and agencies working with children with disabilities.

ADVOCACY, PUBLIC RELATIONS, AND NETWORKING SKILLS

- Promotes an awareness of and support for meeting the library and information needs of all children and the adults who live and work with them.
- Considers the opinions and requests of children, their parents, and service providers.
- Ensures that children with special needs have full access to library materials and services.
- Acts as a liaison with other agencies serving children with disabilities.
- Develops cooperative and collaborative programs among the library, schools, and other provider agencies.
- Utilizes effective public relations techniques and media to promote inclusion in children's library services.
- Understands state, county, and local legal statutes applying to children with special needs.
- Monitors legislation affecting libraries, understands the political process, and advocates on behalf of serving children with special needs.

PROFESSIONALISM AND PROFESSIONAL DEVELOPMENT

- Keeps abreast of current trends, emerging technologies, and research in librarianship and child development and early childhood education, particularly as they relate to children with special needs and their families.
- Demonstrates an understanding of and respect for diversity in cultural and ethnic values and physical and mental abilities.
- Preserves confidentiality in interchanges with patrons.
- Understands that professional development and continuing education are activities to be pursued throughout one's career.

INITIAL STRATEGIES FOR STARTING THE INCLUSION PROCESS

All families come to the library with their own needs, issues, and concerns. Some are typical and shared by most families. Others are unique to individual families. Families of children with disabilities are no different. When looking to include families of children with special needs in the library environment, it may help to use these steps to plan your strategies:

Step 1: Entice families to come to the library.

Step 2: Make families feel comfortable and provide a positive library experience.

Step 3: Make the services and programs developmentally appropriate.

Step 4: Support each family in using library services to the fullest.

Step 5: Expose each family to other community resources and activities.

IDENTIFY THE POPULATION

Before library services and programs can be planned and appropriate materials obtained, it is important to identify the target audience. Several strategies can be used to locate and get to know families of children with disabilities.

Locate Families

1. Contact the school district. Because of confidentiality issues, schools and other agencies are not able to give out names; however, they can provide information about the number, ages, and types of disabilities of the children within the library's service area. Meet with the school personnel assigned to this audience. Ask them for a demographic breakdown or a copy of a community-needs assessment. They may be willing to assist the library in reaching these families by sending a library notice or brochure or organizing a joint meeting.

2. Find out which state agency administers the Early Intervention Program for services to children with disabilities under age three. Check with either the state's Maternal and Child Health Agency, Health Department, or Education Department for referral to the appropriate local agency. The local/regional representative of this agency, as well as the special education department of the local school district for children three to five, will be important contacts and sources of information about local services. They may have access to information about families living in your district. A list of state offices is provided in Appendix C.

3. Network with the early intervention and preschool special education providers serving your community. Explain that the library is expanding services for young children to include those with special needs and hoping to partner with agencies that have expertise and access to families. Chapter 7 offers strategies for collaborating and networking to reach families and children with disabilities, encouraging them to use the library.

4. Talk with parents who are already patrons. They often know of families within the library's service area or may be aware of parent organizations. They may be willing to bring parents who

have a child with a disability to the library or make a connection between the librarian and the family. Chapter 6 discusses how librarians can effectively work with parents.

Find Out about Families

When meeting with professionals or parents, use these questions as a starting point to garner information about the characteristics and needs of families within the library's district.

- How many children have disabilities?
- What types of disabilities are present?
- How might various disabilities affect the stages of child development and age-appropriate practice?
- Do children receive services at an early intervention or preschool special education site, at home, or in some other community-based setting?
- What is a typical day in the life of a family with a young child with a disability?
- When would families be available to come to the library?
- How and where could the library provide outreach to this population?
- What library services do parents want for their children?
- What library services do parents want for themselves?
- If parents of children with disabilities have not been bringing their children to the library, why not?
- What barriers do they perceive?

SET THE TONE

Immediately upon walking into the building, a patron gets a feeling for the atmosphere of the library and attitude of the library staff. To foster an environment that supports inclusion, nurture the following staff behaviors:

Acceptance and Respect. A welcoming atmosphere for families and children with disabilities is a must. Greet them with smiles and the same good customer service provided to all library patrons.

Nonjudgmental Attitude. Apply this attitude to both the child and the parent. For example, if library staff view the parent of a hyperactive child as ineffectual and have a critical attitude that implies, "If I were that child's parent, she would behave," this attitude could undermine a successful inclusionary experience. Staff needs to remain neutral and supportive.

Flexibility. Look beyond policies, procedures, and rules and identify the purposes behind them. Adapt policies to meet the needs of children with disabilities while adhering to the basic intent of the rule or policy.

Awareness and Sensitivity. Be aware of the physical, emotional, and financial demands placed on families of children with special needs. This sensitivity will lead to a more empathetic attitude.

Empathy (Not Sympathy). Feeling sorry for families does nothing to support and empower parents. Offer genuine understanding, caring, and a willingness to partner with the parents and other specialists in the child's life.

Other communication guidelines, while benefiting all children, are particularly critical to keep in mind when working with children with special needs.

- See the child as a child first, the disability only secondarily.
- Always acknowledge the child by speaking directly to her/him. Avoid speaking only to the parent or caregiver as if the child weren't there.
- Be patient. It may take extra time for a child with a disability to say or do things.
- Relax. Don't worry about using common expressions like "See you later" or "I've got to be running along" when talking with children with physical disabilities.
- Use language that refers to the child first and then the disability (e.g., "the boy who is blind" instead of "the blind boy").

Suggestions on how to better communicate with children who have specific disabilities can be found in *Disabilities, Children and Libraries: Mainstreaming Services in Public Libraries and School Library Media Centers* by Linda Lucas Walling and Marilyn H. Karrenbrock. Chapter 6 of this book focuses on understanding and communicating with parents.

BEGIN WHERE STAFF IS MOST COMFORTABLE

For many librarians and support staff, the acquisition of materials for a new collection or the expansion of an existing one may be the most comfortable place to start. Collections can include books, videos, books on tape, magazines, and pamphlets on an array of parenting and disability issues or children's materials in a variety of formats (braille, large print, and tactile books, captioned videos, and adaptive toys). If new acquisitions are not possible, find out what is available within your county or state library system and offer access to materials via interloan. Chapters 9 through 12 focus on collections.

Collection development can often be the first step in the staff's identification with the goals of inclusion. The process of researching, selecting, ordering, processing, and shelving materials that meet the needs of children with disabilities and their families increases staff awareness. Developing brochures and bibliographies can also raise staff awareness and sensitivity. Knowledge of appropriate materials not only provides information to educate staff, but helps to build confidence and increase comfort level when encountering a family with special needs.

PROVIDE A CLIMATE THAT SUPPORTS STAFF AS THEY GO THROUGH THIS PROCESS

Although staff may have difficulties in adapting to these changes, there are ways to set a tone that will make the process easier. Allowing staff to voice their concerns validates their feelings and is critical to the process of accepting and working with families and children with special needs. Before expanding their roles and learning new skills, staff need the opportunity to vent frustrations and anger. This "feeling exchange" is best done in an open forum where as many staff members as possible (not just children's staff) can attend. The forum needs to provide an open atmosphere where staff can share both positive and negative feelings. They must be able to do this honestly and without fear of their job being impacted or how fellow workers, supervisors, and administrators may view them. Having a disabilities specialist or someone trained in early intervention and preschool special education conduct the forum helps set an impartial and nonjudgmental tone. Because they are acknowledged experts and are not in a position to impose change in the library, staff may be more accepting of their suggestions and viewpoints.

Validation of staff feelings is heightened when staff have an opportunity to articulate their concerns to supervisors and explore strategies together. Interdisciplinary teamwork involving many staff members strengthens inter- and intra-agency collaborations, increases the number of people with a vested interest in promoting the process of inclusion, and provides a network of interdisciplinary expertise and resources that team members can draw upon.

Offer this forum regularly. Those who in theory support the concept of inclusion may feel different as they experience real-life challenges. The forum provides an ongoing opportunity for staff to share their frustrations as well as their positive, heartwarming, and inspiring stories. Positive stories about real children and families having successful library experiences are wonderful motivators and morale boosters.

Attitudinal changes take time and patience. When a staff member, who initially expressed anxiety and perhaps even anger, shares a positive experience that influenced the development of the family and the child, other staff can observe the impact of the library's role in the inclusion process. The individual staff member feels personally gratified and supervisory staff can take this opportunity to point out how all staff contributed to this positive development.

In one library, a set of nonverbal, antisocial, two-and-a-half-year-old twins were viewed by staff as "terrors with a permissive mother" when they came into the library. The twins pulled books and toys off the shelf and left the room in complete disarray. The mother paid little attention to them and the disruption they caused, appearing herself to be in need of support and assistance. The librarian realized that this was a complex problem that required intervention.

She listened to her staff's feelings of frustration and provided enough support to handle the extra work the children generated. She spoke to the mother directly about the children's behavior, explaining that they needed supervision and constant assistance and could not be left to roam the library or destroy materials. She suggested that when the children came in, a gate be used to keep the children safely within the early childhood area. She asked that the mother stay in the area with the children and that they pick up the materials along with the staff. She offered her assistance to get additional library materials for the family as needed. This intervention required creative thinking and good communication skills on the part of the librarian.

The family continued to use the library and began to successfully acclimate to the library environment. After several months, one of the children responded to a staff member's greeting by looking directly at her and saying "book" for the first time. The staff member was thrilled. The librarian pointed out how much the entire staff had supported this family during the prior months by their direct or indirect roles in the process. Everyone felt positive and could appreciate the benefits of their new or expanded roles.

PROVIDE TRAINING

Training can be provided in a variety of ways depending on the library's budget, staff size, and need. Keep in mind that the first staff members that patrons often come into contact with are usually not librarians, so all staff need basic training. At the very least, most staff members should be part of a formal American with Disabilities Act training workshop to make them aware of the law and its ramifications for providing library service. Depending on the type and amount of patron interaction, additional training will be needed for successful inclusion.

Training Workshops

Training need not be costly. Look to the community's early intervention or preschool special education professionals for expertise or already existing disability/inclusion oriented training opportunities that may be available in the local area. If the library offers an Employee Assistance Program, access programs they offer or request that a special training workshop be developed and tailored to practicing inclusion.

Individual Self-Directed Training

Staff can be provided with resources to read, view, or listen to on their own or library time. Providing either a formal or informal setting in which they can share and discuss the information and how it may apply to their positions, tends to enhance the effectiveness of the materials read and helps define what is expected of staff. A comprehensive bibliography of resources related to the inclusion of young children with disabilities is included in Appendix A.

Observation of Early Intervention Professionals

Observation combined with information and follow-up discussion provides a rich learning opportunity. Librarians can visit early intervention or preschool special education facilities and simply watch how teachers interact with children of various abilities. Or, arrange for the library to provide meeting room space for a program conducted by early intervention or preschool special education providers for children with special needs and their parents. At such a program, the librarian can provide a display of materials, answer informational questions, and observe parent/child, child/child, teacher/child, and teacher/parent interactions.

Much of the anxiety of not knowing what to do or how to respond in a particular instance when working with children with special needs is lessened if an early intervention professional or preschool special education teacher participates in the library program. Because these providers are looking for natural community settings for their children, they are often very willing to participate in a joint program, modeling for the staff and other families and children in a group setting. Contact local agencies and ask for their assistance.

Train the Trainer

Arrange for key staff members to attend formal trainings and bring the information back to staff in large or small group settings. A team of trainers spanning all positions within the library (page, clerk, paraprofessional, and librarian) can relate training to their particular job responsibilities. They can discuss the interaction of various position responsibilities and how best to work together when assisting families.

PREPARE, INFORM, AND INVOLVE THE COMMUNITY

The entire community needs to be involved in the inclusionary process. Inform the public about your commitment to serve children with special needs. A good place to begin is the library newsletter. Displays, bibliographies, and informational kits highlighting inclusion and children with disabilities are other strategies to increase awareness and make a clear statement about the library's commitment to this process. Sending information to or visiting key organizations in the community are effective in promoting the concept of inclusion. Schools, houses of worship, and fraternal, service, and civic organizations have the potential of reaching many people and are often willing to publicize new community services.

Inclusion is every child's right, but it is also every family's choice. Families cannot make informed choices if they don't know what is available to them. Plan to visit early intervention and preschool special education agencies in your area and inform providers and local health officials of the library's services, programs, and materials and desire to reach out to this audience. Offer to speak to parent groups at local schools serving children with disabilities, and provide meeting room space and materials for parent support groups. Most important, ask them what they want for their children and families and listen with an open mind.

Provide a forum where community members and parents of children with special needs can start a dialogue. Having a parent of a child with disabilities share feelings, concerns, and personal experiences is extremely effective in raising awareness, changing attitudes, and gaining support from community members. The establishment of a community inclusion task force is one strategy that brings together parents and key leaders of a community who are interested and supportive of the concept. Task force members can identify barriers that exist within the community and work together to provide solutions.

Working with families of children with special needs challenges library professionals to explore personal attitudes and develop competencies to better serve special constituencies. Through individual attitude assessment, a commitment to improving skills, an understanding of the audience, and access to training, librarians can begin to develop inclusive practices.

RESOURCES

Deines-Jones, Courtney and Connie Van Fleet. 1995. *Preparing Staff to Serve Patrons with Disabilities: A How-To-Do-It Manual for Librarians.* New York: Neal-Schuman.

Velleman, Ruth A. 1990. *Meeting the Needs of People with Disabilities: A Guide for Librarians, Educators, and Other Service Professionals.* Phoenix: Oryx Press.

Walling, Linda Lucas and Marilyn H. Karrenbrock. 1993. *Disabilities, Children and Libraries: Mainstreaming Services in Public Libraries and School Library Media Centers.* Englewood, Colo.: Libraries Unlimited Inc.

Wright, Keith and Judith F. Davis. 1991. *Serving the Disabled: A How-To-Do-It Manual for Librarians.* New York: Neal-Schuman.

REFERENCES

Association for Library Service to Children. 1989. *Competencies for Librarians Serving Children in Public Libraries.* Chicago: American Library Association.

6 COMMUNICATING WITH PARENTS

Inclusive library service reflects both the individuality of the child and the important role of the family. Partnership and collaboration with parents are essential for the delivery of quality service, particularly when working with children with disabilities. Because librarians have only limited contact, they may not be fully aware of the extent or significance of the child's disability or the degree of stress with which the family is coping. Librarians need to consult and communicate with parents to effectively serve children. It is critical that librarians develop a general sensitivity to the emotional needs of these families, practice active and reflective listening skills, and implement strategies to encourage parents to trust and partner with the library.

When we refer to parents, it is important to remember that the changing status of "family" in today's society is reflected in the array of "groupings" or "units" in which children are raised, ranging from single parent to grandparent to adoptive parent. Many parents work and the child care provider plays a major role in child rearing. Some children are placed in foster care or have a guardian assigned to them. In any case, parents or family, in the context of this book, refers to those persons who consistently serve in caregiving roles for the child.

Even as they acknowledge the importance of family in providing library services to all children, librarians need to understand that parents of children with disabilities have a unique set of emotional and informational needs. These families often become isolated. Sometimes the parents themselves have special problems such as alcoholism, a mental disability, or poverty that put the family under additional stress. Providing service requires greater sensitivity, insight, skills, and knowledge on the part of library staff. Whether the librarian needs to communicate sensitive information about a child's behavior or uncover parents' "real" questions regarding their child's handicapping condition, a basic appreciation for the family's situation will set the tone for inclusion.

UNDERSTANDING THE NEEDS AND FEELINGS OF PARENTS

When parents first learn about their child's disability, they often feel overwhelmed and emotionally unsure. In all their dreams for a child, no parent wants to picture that something could go wrong. For many families, those dreams are shattered when parents learn that their child has a developmental delay or disability. Parents may experience a range of emotions, outlined in *A Family Child Care Provider's Guide* (1996, p. 36), that can recur as the child grows and develops. These include:

Denial and Anger. Parents may believe there is nothing wrong with their child or express anger at the person who has provided information concerning a possible problem.

Grief and Loss. "My child will not grow up to be normal and healthy and therefore all of my expectations of a wonderful family are gone."

Fear. "What is wrong with my child? How can I cope with this problem in my life?"

Guilt. "Did I cause the problem?" or "Why me?" "Why my child?"

Confusion. Parents may not fully understand what is happening and what will happen.

Powerlessness. Parents feel overwhelmed at not being able to change what is happening or exercise any control over the situation.

Disappointment. "My child will not be perfect and, therefore, is less valuable as a person."

Rejection. Parents may reject the child or other family members.

Parents of children with disabilities often feel a sense of isolation from other families. They may have had painful experiences or sensed the fear on the part of other parents to have their "typically developing" children interact with their child who has special needs. They often look to other families who have children with special needs in order to find support and a sense of community.

Even as they experience emotional turmoil, parents seek advice and access to information. Parents often turn to professionals to satisfy these needs. The process of gathering information does not always go smoothly. Parents may be afraid to ask questions or have difficulty putting their concerns into words. They may not ask a question directly or ask it so generally that the question could be viewed strictly as a research inquiry, not as the intensely personal request for information and support that it is. Professionals may not take the time to listen or may minimize concerns in an attempt to reassure an anxious parent.

Information is not the only need of parents of children with disabilities. As with all families, these parents need support in their parenting role. Many families today are separated from their extended families. Professionals and community members are often the only people, outside of their immediate family, who may come in contact with their children. Public librarians who begin to offer services and resources targeted for families and young children may find themselves increasingly sought after to provide this kind of external support to families. Parents will often approach library staff to ask advice about their child's development or how to handle common parenting dilemmas. In addition to general child-rearing concerns, parents of children with special needs may request assistance to help integrate their child into typical library programs or feel that the library should offer programs specially targeted to families and children with disabilities.

PROVIDING INFORMATION AND REFERRAL

Parents of young children often turn to librarians when looking for information about their child's growth and development, emergent literacy and prereading skills, special health and medical concerns, or to locate local resources for their families. The more that libraries open their doors to young children, the more that children's librarians will be called upon to access materials and resources to satisfy the parent's information requests. When working with families of children with disabilities, this need for information may be greatly expanded to include information on specific disabilities as well as community resources to help them with their special needs.

Satisfying a parent's request for services, either through referral to other community resources or by providing services within the library itself, is a primary task of children's librarians who wish to create an inclusive library environment. To make the library a connecting link for families, librarians must continuously build skills, competencies, and a knowledge base to assist them in the development of the parent/professional partnership. Librarians must break down institutional barriers in their efforts to work with other resource professionals and examine their own attitudes toward serving parents. Reviewing the information in Chapter 5 can help staff understand the personal attitudes and behaviors that may negatively or positively affect the creation of an inclusive library environment.

As information and referral specialists, children's librarians need to practice good listening skills, remaining compassionate without becoming overly involved or becoming "family counselors." Being prepared for questions and understanding how to appropriately engage parents in the reference interview process helps to alleviate discomfort or uneasiness while successfully meeting their needs. It is helpful to keep the following guidelines in mind.

Anticipate that parents will ask questions. Be ready for inquiries of a sensitive nature. Provide staff training on how to provide referral information and where such information can be found in the library. Sometimes parents will ask support staff for assistance. Train them on how to assist parents and connect them to the librarian. Having a parents' collection in the children's room, displaying posters and brochures of children with disabilities, and offering an array of services for parents and young children demonstrates to families that the library cares. When parents request help, the library staff needs to be prepared to provide the information that they need.

Be empathetic. Imagine how the parent may be feeling. Conduct the reference interview using reflective listening techniques, restating the parent's question or concern. Be nonjudgmental and verbally communicate support.

Base advice on your qualifications and experience. Although librarians may have degrees and credentials in related fields, it is important to remember that a librarian is not a personal friend, counselor, or social worker. Learn to say, "I'm not the best person to answer that question or solve that problem. Let's see if we can find reading material or a video that can provide some information and I'll be glad to look for someone who is qualified to help you."

Be approachable, but draw boundaries. You can't solve all problems for all families. Tell parents that the library is pleased to assist them with their request. Listen long enough and ask pertinent questions in order to uncover what it is the parent actually wants (e.g., a support group, health information, or a therapeutic service). There may be a support group that already meets in the library or you can refer them to appropriate agencies for help.

Personal boundaries are equally important. It is a delicate line between being a family support professional and a personal friend. Parents sometimes step over the line unintentionally, especially if they are emotionally upset and feel that the librarian is someone who is warm and caring. If the reference interview goes beyond a point that is comfortable, respectfully communicate a limit to the parent.

Become familiar with local resources. Many libraries have compiled a community resource directory either on paper or as part of the online public access catalog (OPAC). It is the responsibility of the children's librarian to ensure that services to families and young children are fully included and that children's staff are trained in the use of the file. Sometimes it is necessary to personally contact referral listings or services that are offered by a local agency. Parents in need often require information fast. Having brochures or a printed list on hand as well as personal knowledge of local services motivates parents to begin the problem-solving process. Chapter 11 provides information on organizing and locating resources within the library and the community.

IDENTIFYING CHILDREN WHO MAY NEED SERVICES

Children's librarians often find themselves observing behaviors in a storytime or parent/child workshop that alert them to the possibility that a particular child may have a delay or disability. A toddler in a workshop who does not show interest in the toys or respond to his mother as other children do, or a prekindergarten child with very limited language, may draw the attention of the librarian. Some children exhibit inappropriate social behavior such as biting or hitting other children or running uncontrollably in a program setting. Others do not seem to learn basic skills such as repeated finger plays and songs, repetitious program patterns, or simple number or letter recognition. Experienced librarians may recognize atypical behavior but often are unsure about how to inform parents. They may even question their responsibility and role in identifying these behaviors and voicing their concerns.

As family service professionals, it is important to remember that we have a responsibility to advocate for children and to intercede on their behalf. The sooner a child's disability is recognized, the greater chance he has to reach his full potential. Early intervention or preschool special education services are critical for the child with special needs. Often family service professionals hesitate to confront a problem with a parent because they are afraid that the parent may become angry or defensive. It is important to remember that, even if parents initially deny the librarian's concerns, when the problem recurs in another setting, the parent may be more ready to accept the information. Or, if the problem recurs in the library setting, the librarian can bring the issue up again, reflecting on past experience. Most parents will welcome your interest and involvement with their child. Oftentimes, they have observed the same behaviors at home and do not know where to turn for advice and help.

PREPARING TO TALK WITH PARENTS

Before approaching parents, it is important to reflect and make notes on the child's behavior. Try to observe the child on more then one occasion. Asking the following questions, taken from *A Family Child Care Provider's Guide* (1996, p. 30), may help to clarify the behaviors that are at issue.

- Is the child too active, or not active enough?
- Is the child's behavior harmful to himself or others?
- Is the social environment frequently disrupted and tense due to the child's behavior?
- Does the child seem to have chronic health problems?
- Does the child have problems with seeing or hearing?
- Is the child talking? Does the child talk differently than other children?
- Does the child seem excessively fearful?
- Does the child consistently withdraw from children, adults, and activities?
- Is the child not rolling, walking, or moving like other children the same age?
- Has the problem or situation persisted over time, or increased in severity, frequency, or noticeability, regardless of trying a variety of strategies for coping?
- Is the child's behavior significantly unusual compared to typical child behavior?

When speaking with parents about their child, librarians need to talk openly and honestly, focusing on the child's behavior. Consider the approach and setting in which the conversation will occur. Handle the discussion discreetly, with care and sensitivity. Here are nine tips for a successful intervention:

1. **Summarize and write down observations of the child.** Use the questions above to guide your observations. If another staff member is in attendance, ask the person for assistance in identifying their observations of the child's atypical behavior or development as well. Using written documentation, even in simple note

form, makes it easier to clarify specific behaviors and helps keep the conversation on target.

2. **Focus on the behavior of the child.** Describe what the child is doing or not doing. Never make an attempt to diagnose problems or make judgments about the child.

3. **Determine in advance the major points.** Plan what to say and how to say it. Speaking confidentially with another staff member before talking with the parent may help to clarify the issues.

4. **Stress that the parent is the child's primary teacher.** Reaffirm that as the child's first and primary teachers parents know their child best. Listen carefully to the explanation of why a child may be behaving a certain way.

5. **Anticipate a parent's range of reactions.** There is a wide range of emotions that parents may have when first approached. Review the section in this chapter on emotions that parents may feel about their children, particularly if there is a disability or a delay.

6. **Try not to get defensive.** It is common for parents to initially deny the problem, resent the intrusion, or blame the staff. This is when written notes summarizing specific behaviors will come in handy.

7. **Listen to the parents carefully.** Review the guidelines on active listening skills in the latter part of this chapter. If parents express similar concerns, be prepared to provide information and referral or suggest a possible solution to improve the child's participation within the library program. If a parent feels there is no problem, suggest to the parent that they may wish to ask another professional or read an article or book.

8. **Avoid these discussions when a child is present.** It is inappropriate and demeaning to talk about a child with the child present, except to praise. Do not discuss problems or concerns unless you are alone with the parents. Maybe the child could be taken care of by the support staff for a short period of time or consider phoning the parents at home and asking for a good time to speak with them.

9. **Respect confidentiality.** Confidentiality is a must. Discussing children in front of or with other parents is *never* appropriate. Being respectful of parents and building trust are primary considerations for the librarian.

The process of communicating with parents, particularly around sensitive issues regarding their own children, requires flexibility and sensitivity. Being able to communicate effectively is essential. When librarians practice healthy communication skills on a daily basis with parents and adult caregivers, they will be better prepared to constructively handle problem situations when they arise. They will be more secure in their roles as family support professionals and, in difficult situations, be able to turn to other professionals for advice and help.

DEVELOPING LISTENING SKILLS

The most important communication technique when working with families is the ability to listen. Listening improves communication, conveys a caring attitude, and helps the listener to better understand and be in control of a situation. Good listening enables librarians to provide better and more accurate assistance.

Listening is more than hearing. Hearing is a physical act. Listening is an intellectual and emotional act. Hearing acknowledges sounds. Listening requires understanding what is said, getting the whole message, that which is beyond just the words. Active listening is a learned activity.

Effective listening skills do not come naturally. To be an active listener requires practice. Here are five steps to active listening, adapted from *Listen Up: Hear What's Really Being Said* (Dugger, 1991):

1. **Listen to the content.** Being prepared and motivated to listen puts you in the right frame of mind. Listen to what the patron is saying in terms of facts and ideas. Reflecting back to the patron the information he is trying to impart increases understanding. Strive for accuracy.

2. **Listen to the intent.** Use intuition to "hear" the underlying messages, particularly the emotional meaning of what the patron is saying.

3. **Assess the patron's nonverbal communication.** Read and interpret what the patron is "saying" with body language and other nonverbal signals.

4. **Monitor your nonverbal communication and emotional filters.** Be aware of the messages that you may be sending though body language and expressions. Be aware of personal emotional filters that may be affecting your understanding of the message.

5. **Listen to the patron nonjudgmentally and with empathy.** Put yourself in the patron's shoes and try to understand what is shaping his or her feelings. Do not prejudge the patron.

Applying these listening steps when working with parents of children with special needs will help librarians become better information specialists. By listening, librarians will more accurately interpret a parent's information needs. By listening, librarians can lessen the parent's anxiety. By being aware of their own nonverbal communication and emotional filters, librarians can control their own tendencies and diffuse a difficult situation. This awareness and sensitivity sets the stage for librarians to partner with parents and helps them begin the process of acquiring resources, services, and supports for the child.

BUILDING A PARENT/PROFESSIONAL PARTNERSHIP

Establishing positive one-on-one communication with parents is by far the most important building block in the creation of parent/professional partnerships. When working with families, it is also essential to recognize that the attitudes and beliefs that professionals bring to the partnership influence the relationship. To be effective, librarians need to acknowledge their personal feelings about parental responsibility, accept parents as individuals and adult learners, and assess their professional beliefs about serving children within the family unit. Reviewing the following questions, adapted from "Involving Families in Advisory Roles" (1994, p. 5), can help librarians uncover their feelings and opinions regarding their role as family support professionals.

- Do I work to create an environment in which families feel supported and comfortable enough to speak freely?
- Do I listen respectfully to the opinions of family members?
- Do I believe that families' perspectives and opinions are as important as those of professionals?
- Do I consistently value the insights of parents?
- Do I believe that parents can look beyond their own child's and family's experiences?
- Do I clearly state what is expected of families in the library setting?
- Do I understand the demands placed upon parents and how these may affect their performance?
- Do I believe that families bring a unique expertise to the parent/professional relationship?
- Do I believe in the importance of family participation in decision making at the program level?
- Do I believe that parents bring critical elements to library services that no one else can provide?

VIEWING PARENTS AS ADULT LEARNERS

Providing information to parents and developing the parent/professional partnership requires that librarians understand the parent as an adult learner. Adult learners learn at their own pace and in their own styles. They want to incorporate their own knowledge about themselves and their child, preferring a facilitated exchange of ideas rather than a didactic or professorial exchange. Librarians should be prepared that there are times they will provide information that parents will choose to ignore.

Librarians need to be flexible and creative in the parent/professional information exchange. Being comfortable with a wide array of materials and community resources enhances the exchange and provides the librarian with alternative strategies to satisfy the information need. Some parents may be looking for a support group, others are more comfortable researching information on the Internet. Reading a book or short article may be just what is needed by another parent. It is incumbent upon the librarian to be knowledgeable about alternative learning styles and to analyze carefully what resource a particular parent would most readily utilize.

WELCOMING CULTURALLY DIVERSE FAMILIES

In communicating with parents, librarians need to recognize the role that culture, ethnicity, race, religion, gender, and sexual orientation plays in parenting and child rearing. The first step in working with a diverse constituency is to scrutinize one's own feelings and beliefs about groups other than one's own. Acknowledging stereotypes and biases is essential to being able to effectively work with *all* families. Cultural orientation may influence how families interact within the library environment as manifested in

- child-rearing techniques;
- language and communication styles;
- how people seek assistance;
- availability of extended family and informal helping networks;
- attitude toward bureaucracies and government-sponsored programs and services;
- familiarity with American culture.

A diverse staff, reflective of the community that the library serves, is in the best position to meet the needs of a diverse constituency. It is essential for librarians to be aware of and educated about the array of cultures that make up their constituency. Having a good collection of materials targeted to diverse audiences, displaying posters that depict the diversity of our society, being familiar with community resources for a variety of groups, and developing cooperative programs with agencies that work with diverse cultures are just some ideas for including these families within the library setting.

RECOGNIZING PARENTS WITH SPECIAL NEEDS

Parents with substance abuse problems or those who have a mental disability, teenage parents, and families who live in poverty are just some of the families considered at high risk for having children with developmental disabilities. Working with parents with special needs may require another level of understanding and commitment, outside of the scope and educational experience of the children's services staff. When librarians encounter a child whose parent appears to have a mental disability or other form of disability that seems to interfere with the ability to nurture the child's development, a referral to the local early intervention program or preschool special education program would be in the best interest of both the child and parent.

Children of alcohol- or drug-addicted parents can develop problems in interpersonal relationships as a response to impaired parental functions. In the environment in which these children exist, their needs may be ignored and there are often overwhelming external stresses: crime; violence; poverty; drugs; substandard housing; lack of transportation, education, and jobs. Children whose feelings are consistently ignored or rejected, even abused, may learn not to trust or feel (Girard and Kaplan, 1994, p. 23).

In order to reach out to these children, whose families are not likely to use the library, it is necessary for librarians to work in partnership with other local agencies and organizations. Often it is only in close partnership with community-based agencies and through unique strategies like home visitation programs, that libraries can seek to support children and families at highest risk.

Teenage parents present another set of challenges for librarians. Working with teen parents can be difficult because the young parents' own needs often overwhelm their ability to focus on their child's needs. Lack of transportation and motivation may inhibit their interest or ability to bring their child to library programs. Successful programs usually are conducted in collaboration with a local agency that already serves these teenagers, so that agency staff can work with both the teens and the library staff and facilitate their coming to the library. Sometimes librarians can go off-site, bringing resources to the teen parents and their children. Providing books and resources for the professionals who work with teen parents is another strategy for assisting teen parents.

The risks to children of parents with special needs can be minimized by proper intervention designed to support the parents in caring for their children. Prevention and intervention strategies designed at the community level in agencies such as public libraries can aid these children in their struggle to grow into healthy adults. Librarians need to acknowledge that library programs and resources provide a preventive strategy to families and young children in need of healthy role models and appropriate learning environments. For young children, story-hours and library visits may present an opportunity to learn and practice positive social interactions.

ADVOCATING FOR CHILDREN AND FAMILIES

As librarians become comfortable with parents and begin to see the benefits of working with them to help children, they often take on a more proactive stance in their work. As they involve themselves with the broader community of family support professionals, they usually find that their own self-esteem is raised and the library's image is enhanced through their efforts. This enhances their role and reinforces their responsibility both within the library setting and in the community.

Working as advocates on behalf of children and families, it is important for librarians to adopt specific goals and objectives within their own libraries. There are some very definite ways to develop family-centered and inclusive libraries.

Expand the constituency of children's services to include parents. Children's librarians need to advocate for this service strategy. Work with the administration and adult services department to articulate why it is so important for the children's services department to integrate service to parents as part of their mission.

Provide parent support and education. Parent programs need to maintain a balanced focus on the needs of both the parent and child. Focus on the social context of parenthood by strengthening parents' social networks and community ties, as well as assisting parents to increase their parenting skills. Develop parent resource collections in the children's room.

Look for new opportunities to involve families. Be vigilant and flexible in identifying opportunities to work with other agency professionals to develop cooperative programs and services. Encourage parent participation through one-on-one interactions at the children's reference desk and by honoring parents' requests for materials.

Recognize parents as consumers of library service. Parents should be involved in the development of services for themselves and their children. Conduct parent focus groups or form an advisory committee. Distribute evaluation and suggestion forms regularly.

Identify and recruit families. Make the library a visible community resource for families through publicity and networking with local agencies. Encourage other professionals to visit and become knowledgeable about library services.

Tailor programs to the needs and characteristics of the population being served. Targeting diverse audiences and developing new outreach strategies is necessary if libraries wish to broaden their usage base. Appeal to families from a variety of ethnic and socioeconomic backgrounds.

Acquire training for children's services staff on building community collaborations and partnerships. Learning to work collaboratively requires new skills. Ask for help from community agencies with expertise in working with parents. Chapter 7 describes the process of building collaborations in detail.

Becoming allies of the family and forming partnerships with parents will improve services for children both within the library setting and in the community at large. This partnership essentially shifts the paradigm of children's services in public libraries from service for children to service for families. It is critical that librarians recognize their particular role in the partnership and nurture its development, particularly when reaching out to include families and children with special needs.

REFERENCES

Dugger, Jim. 1991. *Listen Up: Hear What's Really Being Said.* Shawnee Mission, Kans.: National Press Publications, a division of Rockhurst College Continuing Education Center.

A Family Child Care Provider's Guide to New York's Early Intervention Program: Trainer's Manual. 1996. Albany, N.Y.: Early Intervention Program, New York State Department of Health.

Frank, Mary, ed. 1983. *Children of Exceptional Parents*. New York: The Haworth Press.

Girard, Judith L. and Lisa Kaplan.1994. *Strengthening High-Risk Families: A Handbook for Practitioners*. New York: Lexington Books.

"Involving Families in Advisory Roles: Eight Steps to Success." 1994. In *Essential Allies* volume of *Advances in Family-Centered Care*. Washington, D.C.: Institute for Family Centered Care.

7 COLLABORATING FOR SUCCESS

WHAT IS COLLABORATION?

Successful collaboration to promote inclusion requires that librarians form a team with parents and other professionals committed to young children with special needs. This collaboration rests on each partner's commitment to share authority, resources, and responsibility in order to create a shared vision and joint goals regarding the inclusion of children with disabilities in the library setting. It demands teamwork and a mutual belief in the following values:

- The family is the primary context in which a child develops.
- Young children with disabilities have more similarities with their nondisabled peers than dissimilarities.
- Inclusion of young children with disabilities in regular community programs is a positive and beneficial experience for all involved.
- Collaboration between families, librarians, service providers, and other community program personnel enhances outcomes for young children with special needs and their families.

For these collaborations to succeed, members need to rely on each other's strengths while recognizing their individual and institutional needs. This process begins with assessing resources. Partners must evaluate the personnel, skills, services, and materials they can share to make the child and the family's library experience successful. They must identify potential problems and issues as well.

In order to ensure participation in library activities, staff must identify not only the library's resources but the outside help they are going to need to make inclusion work. Parents must identify the specific needs of their children in the library setting. Once the shared vision and each partner's strengths and needs have been identified, the team is ready to build inclusive services, comfortable for the partners and welcoming for families.

COMPETENCIES AND SKILLS NEEDED TO BUILD COLLABORATIONS

Working collaboratively on an inclusion team requires certain competencies and skills on the part of library staff. To be successful, it is critical that team members are flexible, innovative and creative, able to identify and work through areas of conflict, and willing to work as part of a team. They must have knowledge of the library's boundaries and the librarian's realm of authority within those boundaries. They also need proficiency in communication, team building and group facilitation, problem solving, and evaluation.

While librarians already possess many of these qualities and competencies, collaborations require a deeper level of commitment to solve problems in territory that may be unfamiliar and uncomfortable. For example, the early intervention or preschool special education providers of a collaborative team may serve children from a number of library districts, but the library can only serve families who reside in its particular district. It is the librarian's responsibility to know this library policy, understand whether or not there is any flexibility regarding the policy, communicate the library's boundaries to the collaborative team, and develop strategies that would keep the library component in the collaborative program while respecting the library's residency limit.

HOW TO BUILD COLLABORATIVE SERVICES

Building collaborative services requires a cyclical planning process that addresses who the partners on the collaborative team will be, how often the team will meet, who will take responsibility for specific activities, and how success will be measured and outcomes evaluated. This process can be divided into five phases. Although described as discrete, linear entities, in reality these phases often blend and recur throughout the inclusion team's time spent together. Although the process is initiated under one set of assumptions, these assumptions are often redefined over time and through communication and evaluation.

The five phases to building collaborative services are

1. Recognizing the goals and boundaries of each party involved;

2. Identifying the types of adaptations and interventions needed by the child;
3. Determining the team's skills and resources;
4. Establishing ongoing communication;
5. Establishing informal and formal evaluation.

PHASE ONE: RECOGNIZE GOALS AND BOUNDARIES

Each partner on the inclusion team may have a set of goals for the child, parameters that define their work with the child and family, and institutional or professional regulations (policies and procedures to which they must adhere). Understanding and respecting the goals and boundaries of each partner is critical to the team's success.

Families

Of primary importance is the family's goals for the child and themselves when using the library. What arc likely goals for families? The list is as varied as the families themselves. Here are some typical goals, which have been identified through interviews with families of children with disabilities:

- I want my child to participate in the library's programming along with my other children.
- I want my child to learn to read.
- I want my child to have playmates.
- I want my child's sibling to see that his brother or sister is a person who can be liked by others.
- I need to learn more about my child's disabilities.
- I need help in identifying emergency services and informing them of my child's disabilities in case I should ever need to call upon them.
- I need help in reminding myself that a piece of equipment or toy doesn't always have to be "adaptive" to be used by my child.
- I need to feel less isolated.
- I need someone who will talk to me and talk to my child.
- I need someone who can show me options and give my child choices.

Families of children with special needs are bound by many commitments. Attending library programs on a regular basis may be difficult. In addition to a typical family's schedule of work, church participation, siblings' activities, daily household chores, and personal needs, families of children with disabilities often have special requirements. The child's medical condition may require frequent doctors' and other specialists' appointments. The child's intervention services or daily school-based programs may severely limit the amount of time that the family can use the library. Some boundaries are personal, such as fear or intimidation about bringing the child to the library.

Getting to know the family and the individual goals it has for its child will help staff to understand what and how library resources can be most effectively utilized. Maybe specific library activities can be consolidated within the child's IFSP or IEP. Or, the librarian may be able to redefine a library program to fit the goals outlined in the child's existing plan. The more familiar partners become with the library and the more familiar librarians become with the family, the more connections the team will make between the child's goals and the library's resources.

Librarians

Once the family's goals and boundaries are defined and understood, it is important to outline the goals and boundaries of the librarian. Here are some likely goals that librarians may have:

- I want to help this child learn to read and to foster reading as a source of lifelong enjoyment.
- I want to assist this parent with accessing information and referral to other community services.
- I want to include young children with special needs and their families in the library's regularly offered programs for young children.
- I want to implement family-centered principles in the library and see the collaborative process as an opportunity to start.
- I want to reach out to families who have not used library services before.
- I want to fulfill my obligation under the Americans with Disabilities Act.
- I want to serve *all* families in my library district.
- I want to work with those providers who serve children in the community.

Boundaries for the librarian may include

- the need to follow library policy, such as a requirement to limit service to district patrons (only families residing within predetermined geographic boundaries) while other cooperating agencies on the inclusion team serve a broader geographic area;
- the need to adhere to library regulations as they relate to borrowing materials, hours of operation, program registration, liability, funding, and general service provision;

- the need to maintain a balance in the allocation of resources for the various age groups served;
- the need to adhere to a predetermined budget that has little flexibility to meet unanticipated expenses.

In addition to family and library goals and boundaries, there will be the goals and boundaries of other service providers working with the family. Their goals are child specific and are determined by the child's IFSP or IEP. They must coordinate their goals for the child who wishes to attend library programs with those goals that have been approved in the plans for the child. Fortunately, many IFSPs and IEPs include statements that are broad enough, in terms of inclusion in community programs, to authorize providers' work with librarians and the integration of library activities in plans for the child. Two examples illustrate how the level of providers' effectiveness is influenced by boundaries outlined in the plans.

A mother of a two year old, who is deaf, wanted her son to participate in library programming. The early intervention service coordinator, who helped the mother develop the IFSP, included library activities as part of the child's plan. A teacher of the deaf and hearing impaired was assigned to the family and was thereby authorized to attend meetings, develop strategies, and offer services in the library setting, using the child, family, and librarian to implement the goals. She brought the boy to storytime and attended the Parent/Child Workshop with the family. The boy, his family, his teacher, and the library staff became familiar and comfortable with each other.

In contrast, consider a little girl who is four and receiving therapy under an IEP, using the services of a physical therapist. In this instance, when the team designed the child's plan, the physical therapist was directed to work on goals and objectives specifically outlined in the IEP and related to the child's educational performance. The family and the child's team failed to articulate their goal for inclusion and only the child's motor goals, related to her future academic performance in kindergarten, were included. The physical therapist was, therefore, not authorized to attend meetings with the inclusion team or advise the library staff. She could only offer written suggestions. These boundaries limited the degree of outside assistance that could be provided by the physical therapist, minimized the integration of library resources in the girl's learning experiences, and affected the team's effectiveness at increasing the child's inclusion in the community.

PHASE TWO: IDENTIFY ADAPTATIONS AND INTERVENTIONS

The second phase in collaborating with families and service providers is to identify the types of adaptations and interventions that the child requires and the family would like to see occur. This must be handled with great sensitivity. The inclusion team must help the family articulate their desires, expecting that parents may be ambivalent.

Some families feel comfortable using any adaptation or intervention necessary to facilitate their child's participation in community services. They feel comfortable with the use of equipment, aids, and other accommodations that satisfy the child's needs. Other families want their child to participate in programming without special attention being drawn to the child's disability. They want to separate "school" and family life, allowing their child the opportunity to be accepted without undue notice of the disability. They want their child to be treated like every other child in the program. Often, their desires and reality may be in conflict and the family may need time to decide what interventions and adaptations they want. Obviously, an adaptation that does not single out the child with special needs and yet facilitates the child's participation is ideal. Exploring various possibilities with families will earn their respect and demonstrate a collaborative family-centered approach.

PHASE THREE: DETERMINE TEAM SKILLS AND RESOURCES

Determining which team member has the skills, time, and resources to accomplish the desired objective or goal is the next phase of building collaborative services. This process requires honesty, patience, and a willingness to identify and share resources. The following scenario is a good example of this process.

The mother of Tommy, a kindergartner who has cerebral palsy, approached the children's librarian and stated she wanted to enroll him in the library's Reading Buddies Club with his best friend, Matthew. The Reading Buddies Club is a storytime program that children attend without their parents. A significant part of the Reading Buddies program is an art activity that relates to the stories being read. After talking with Tommy's mother, the librarian asked if she and the child's teacher could meet with the library staff to discuss how they could best serve Tommy.

The collaborative inclusion team, comprised of the mother, the librarian, and the teacher, identified four issues that had to be addressed in order for Tommy to participate in the program.

1. Tommy needed help in moving his wheelchair and participating in the craft project. Though he was able to move his arms and hands, he had particular difficulty with fine motor skills.

2. Tommy suffered from petit mal seizures. He was on medication that controlled the seizures but on rare occasions he experienced attacks that required repositioning him.

3. Only one librarian was assigned to the program. She felt that she could not attend to Tommy's needs and keep the other 18 youngsters in the group involved. She wanted Tommy to participate but was concerned that she would not be able to accommodate the child.

4. The mother preferred that Tommy attend the sessions without her. She felt her presence would bring additional attention to Tommy and interfere with his peer relationships, adding to his sense of isolation. In addition, she would like the opportunity to talk with other adults and parents while Tommy is occupied.

After careful discussion among the inclusion team members, the team developed several strategies to address these issues. Each partner contributed time, expertise, and resources so that Tommy could be included.

- Tommy's mother spoke to the parents of Matthew, Tommy's best friend, to request Matthew's assistance in pushing Tommy's wheelchair in the library and assisting him with the craft projects.
- Tommy's mother trained the librarian in the simple positioning techniques that her son required if he had a seizure. She agreed to remain in the library in case she was needed in an emergency.
- The librarian reexamined the types of crafts presented in the Reading Buddies Club and replaced some of the more complicated activities with ones that required less use of fine motor skills.
- The special education teacher rearranged her sessions with Tommy so that one session, every other week, was conducted during the library program. She served as a resource to the librarian and offered to help the librarian adapt the craft projects in small ways so that Tommy could better participate.

PHASE FOUR: ESTABLISH ONGOING COMMUNICATION

Fine-tuning the collaborative process with ongoing communication helps develop the shared vision that is necessary for successful inclusion. Team members must communicate on a regular basis. Roles of each partner must be clearly understood. This is not something that can simply be left to chance. One member of the inclusion team needs to assume a leadership role to ensure ongoing communication through phone calls, simple notes, or meetings about the adaptations and interventions instituted. Who this person will be is dependent on the composition of the inclusion team. If the program or activity is written into a child's IFSP or IEP, a member of the early intervention or preschool special education team will most likely take the lead in communicating with the family, the service providers, and the library staff.

Many factors influence how and with whom the librarian needs to communicate. If the librarian planning the program is not the same person who will be conducting the program, it is imperative that these two people communicate in detail about the child's behavior, program content, and/or alternative strategies that need to be employed. It is also important for the library staff, the service providers, and the parent to communicate before and after each program session to plan and assess their collaborative efforts. Preprogram planning among all the parties tends to be scheduled and formal while postprogram meetings tend to be more informal and take place immediately following a program. If changes or adaptations are necessary, the service providers and parents need to communicate these changes to the service coordinator (if one is part of the inclusion team). The program librarian needs to do the same with her supervisor. Throughout the process, it is critical that team members are in accord on the goals of the child's inclusionary experience and are working together to accomplish these goals.

When a child is receiving services as part of the early intervention or special education system, parents may request that these services be delivered in the library setting. In this case, the parent needs to first speak with the early intervention or preschool professionals, who would then contact the librarian. Librarians need to openly discuss the situation with the service providers and the child's parents. If delivered at the library, services can be provided within the children's room or as part of an established library program.

Sometimes a parent, independent of the child's individual service plan, requests that her child be included in library programs. The librarian should inform the parent about activities that are available and stress the library's willingness to work with the family and the child's service providers to ensure that the child's library experience will be a positive one. If the parent expresses concern about her child's ability to participate fully in an activity, the librarian needs to explore possible adaptations. This exploration may require only the parent and librarian to arrive at a solution. Or, it could require the expertise of the child's service provider or an early intervention specialist. Examples of adaptations to typical library programs and activities are covered in Chapter 8.

If the child is not receiving early intervention or preschool special education services and the parent is interested in exploring such services, the librarian can refer the parent to the appropriate agency and provide written materials to help the parent define their particular need.

Some libraries provide a packet designed specifically for families concerned about the development of their young child. These packets include materials on child development and a list of referrals. For many families, this is their first exposure to the existence and availability of such services. This type of interchange can lead to the development of an inclusion team, particularly if the parent does seek and get services for her child. Chapter 6 discusses communicating with parents and referral skills. Chapter 11 provides information on Early Intervention Kits for Families.

PHASE FIVE: ESTABLISH ONGOING EVALUATION

In the majority of cases, the inclusion team will choose an informal and ongoing evaluation process that can be used when any member encounters difficulty. The analysis of immediate actions is far easier than examining those which have occurred days or weeks earlier. If librarians approach parents for feedback after each session, in a casual and supportive way, parents will most likely react in a positive manner. New options can be explored immediately by evaluating situations as they occur and preventing small problems from growing into bigger ones. A few moments to converse and reflect may be all that is necessary to gain perspective on alternative strategies.

For more difficult situations, it may be necessary to put special time aside to evaluate. Librarians may need to brainstorm with colleagues, parents, and other professionals. Or, the librarian may wish to consult with the early intervention or preschool special education professional involved with the child and family. Often a simple modification to the activity or approach is all that is required to make the inclusion experience a successful one. It is important to remember that each partner on the inclusion team wants the child with special needs to be successful.

REAL EXAMPLES OF COLLABORATIONS IN ACTION

Time for Twos
Just Kids Diagnostic and Treatment Center (Suffolk County, N.Y.), an integrated child care facility that includes infants, toddlers, and preschoolers with special needs, received a grant in 1992 to provide services in natural community settings, particularly those with a parent/child focus. Because of a long history of cooperation and partnership with the Mastics-Moriches-Shirley Community Library, Just Kids

knew that the library already offered a program, the Parent/Toddler Workshop, which met the grant's objectives.

After multiple planning sessions and extensive communication among the early intervention providers and librarians, a strategy was developed to integrate five families of children with special needs into the library's Parent/Toddler program. While some modifications were made regarding registration procedures (slots were specifically set aside for the Just Kids families) and attendance rules (families were allowed to attend twice as many sessions), the basic goals, objectives, and structure of the workshop remained intact.

It was a win/win experience for all. The library was pleased with the opportunity to involve the families of children with disabilities who probably would not have participated in the workshop, and Just Kids, through its partnership with the library, was able to provide an inclusive experience for families enrolled at their center. Most of all, the children and families had a successful, fun experience in their community, bringing them into contact with other families and introducing them to library resources.

Partners for Inclusion
In 1994, the Middle Country Public Library and the Mastics-Moriches-Shirley Community Library participated in the design and implementation of the Partners for Inclusion Project, in collaboration with the Suffolk County Department of Health Services, Just Kids Diagnostic and Treatment Center, Developmental Disabilities Institute, and Dowling College. Funded by a grant from the New York State Department of Health, the goals of the project were threefold: to expand the delivery of early intervention services in natural environments in Suffolk County; to raise the awareness among the communities-at-large regarding inclusion; to help families of young children with developmental disabilities participate in community activities of their choosing.

Both libraries offer an array of family-centered, early childhood programs and are firmly established and well respected as collaborative partners. Two part-time family specialists were hired for the project, using the libraries as their home base. Their primary job was to outreach to families of young children with disabilities and encourage involvement in community activities, using the library as the starting point. A community inclusion task force was formed in each library district to identify community barriers to successful inclusion and to develop strategies to overcome these barriers.

The libraries established special services, in conjunction with their inclusion team partners, to attract families of children with disabilities. An adaptive toy-lending library was established at each site. Parent support groups were formed. Children from the local early childhood service sites (Just Kids and the Developmental Disabilities Institute) were registered for regular library programs and attended them with their service providers. A variety of other programs were developed jointly by the library staffs and the participating early intervention providers. To date, the libraries continue to promote the inclusion of children with disabilities in library programs. Further information on this model demonstration project is available in *Partners for Inclusion: Welcoming Infants and Toddlers with Disabilities and Their Families into Community Activities: A Replication Guide.* Chapter 10 discusses how to set up a toy-lending library.

Regardless of who initiates the process, the formation of an inclusion team that includes the parent, librarian, and early intervention or preschool special education professional can be an effective way to ensure a child's ability to participate in library services and programs. In most cases, libraries are not thought of when a child's plans are drawn up or teams are formed. It is incumbent upon librarians to actively reach out and partner with providers and families and find ways for these families to access services. Encouraging greater awareness of the resources the library has to offer and its potential as part of the inclusion process can only be successfully implemented through this proactive and collaborative stance.

RESOURCES

Cohen, Larry, Nancy Baer, and Pam Satterwhite. 1994. *Developing Effective Coalitions: An Eight-Step Guide.* Pleasant Hill, Calif.: Contra Costa County Health Services Prevention Program.

Feinberg, Sandra and Sari Feldman. 1996. *Serving Families and Children through Partnerships: A How-To-Do-It Manual for Librarians.* New York: Neal-Schuman.

Melaville, A. I. and M. J. Blank. 1991. *What It Takes: Structuring Interagency Partnerships to Connect Children and Families with Comprehensive Services.* Washington, D.C.: The Education and Human Service Consortium.

A Model for Collaboration. 1993. *Success by Six.* Syracuse, N.Y.: United Way. *Partners for Inclusion: Welcoming Infants and Toddlers with Disabilities and Their Families into Community Activities: A Replication Guide.* 1997. Hauppauge, N.Y.: Suffolk County Department of Health Services.

8 GUIDELINES FOR ADAPTING YOUR LIBRARY

Librarians know more than they realize about meeting the needs of children with disabilities. Their ability to adapt services to a wide variety of audiences and their public service orientation are trademarks of their daily work. As children's services specialists, they design recreational and educational programs for children within a broad range of ages. Individualized, rather than group learning, is the norm. For children with disabilities, being in an environment where they do not have to achieve some measurable objective or concentrate on remediating some skill is an opportunity—one not often experienced—that libraries offer. Fun, a sense of belonging, and participation are primary objectives for inclusive library practice.

Many parents of children with disabilities come to the library precisely because they want a normal community experience for their child. They are not looking for therapy and, if they ever did consider having therapy provided in the library, it would not be the librarian who would provide it. Because library activities are typically nonstructured and self-selected, they are ideally suited for children with varying abilities and interests. Within this framework, it is essential for librarians to see the child first and consider the disability only if some accommodation needs to be made to enable the child to participate in a desired activity.

GENERAL CONSIDERATIONS

The most critical factor in providing a successful library experience for a child with a disability is the behavior of the librarian and staff. Other children (and their parents) will take their cue from the enthusiasm, sensitivity, and comfort level of the staff as they acknowledge, accept, and even welcome individual differences among children. Be prepared to answer children's questions openly and honestly, using simple, matter-of-fact language. Emphasize how we are all alike as well as how we are different.

Special skills or training are not necessarily required to provide a positive library experience for a child with a disability. Children are children first. See their strengths and commonalities foremost; the disabilities secondarily. Initially assume the child can participate and only consider ways of adapting the environment or the activity to permit the child to experience success. If adaptations are necessary, think creatively, starting first with knowledge of typical development.

Remember that parents and other professionals working with the child are in the best position to recommend any needed modifications. First observe and then consult with parents. In some instances, parents may hesitate to identify that their child has a disability. They may have had negative experiences or anticipate a negative reaction. They may be fearful for their child's safety or anxious that their child will be teased or not allowed to participate. Refer to Chapter 6 for further strategies on partnering and communicating with parents.

THE ENVIRONMENT

A safe, developmentally appropriate, child-centered environment is essential for providing a successful inclusionary experience. Materials, programs, and activities that encourage and support typical development and provide opportunities for play and socialization will provide the basic elements of service for all young children, including those with disabilities. Adaptations do not necessarily mean major changes in routines but merely ways for an individual child to participate in an activity or program based on their individual needs. Most accommodations are simply good practice.

While assessing the library's environment, it is best not only to look at accommodations but to consider how the environment welcomes children with disabilities. Ask the following questions while taking a walk from the entrance of the building into and around the children's room.

1. Are all areas of the facility physically accessible to the child?
2. Are pathways open, clear, and wide enough to accommodate wheelchairs or strollers?
3. Are floors made of tile or wood and perhaps slippery to someone using a cane or walker?
4. Are carpeted floors free of wrinkles, rips, curled corners, or loose bindings that could present a danger to someone physically or visually challenged?
5. Does the height of the computer stations, catalogs, activity centers, or tables present any barriers, keeping in mind that a wheelchair for a child is smaller than for an adult?
6. Is the children's room free of loose rugs and clutter, at least in the walkways?
7. Are all areas, including program areas, well lit?
8. Are signs in clear, large print, with print in distinct contrast from the background color? Has the library considered accompanying picture cues?
9. Does the room reflect an inclusionary philosophy? Look at

the posters, pictures, book displays, dolls, etc. Do they reflect diversity and help children learn about disabilities?

10. Is there a variety of age-appropriate materials to accommodate children of different interests and abilities?

11. Are there areas for more quiet, individual activities as well as other areas for more active, social play so children and parents can select activities most suitable to their needs?

Do not forget the typical considerations for any children's room: safety plugs on electrical outlets, computer wires secured safely out of reach, seating and shelving at lower levels with materials easily accessible by children. *Learning Environments for Young Children: Rethinking Library Spaces and Services* (S. Feinberg, J. Kuchner, and S. Feldman, Chicago: ALA Editions, 1998) provides an in-depth description of the essential elements of library-based early childhood service. Checklists on the physical and social environment outline basic requirements.

PROGRAMS AND POLICIES

Since adaptations can be made in many ways, flexibility is the underlying principle in making library programs accessible to children with disabilities. Think simply and creatively (costly and complicated adaptations are not necessary). Sometimes this means looking at materials already at hand in a new way. Appropriate toys, for instance, can often be used by children in different ways and at different developmental levels. Providing sponges for a child with tactile sensitivity to encourage him or her to participate in a "finger painting" activity is a simple, imaginative adaptation that requires little cost and no extra staff time or training. To be inclusive, consider the following adaptation guidelines:

- Be willing to adjust age and other requirements to make an appropriate program placement.
- Keep in mind that it is usually advisable to have children of the same chronological age remain together whenever possible.
- Eliminate any program eligibility requirements that would have the effect of screening out children with disabilities.
- Suggest to parents that they may want to adjust their arrival or departure time. Arriving early may help a child get acclimated to the surroundings and achieve a certain comfort level before the larger group of parents and children arrive. Leaving early or gradually extending the amount of time a child participates can make a program successful for the child with a short attention span.
- Permit parents to accompany their child into programs, even

those designed "for children only." Encourage parents to separate only if they feel comfortable doing so.

- Be open to the possibility that the parent may want to bring a child's service provider into a library program. The service provider may want to work with the child within the context of an experience that is part of the child's regular routine. Or, the service provider may want to give the parent or the library staff suggestions on ways for the child to participate in the program more fully. This can be a wonderful opportunity for library staff to learn from the expertise of a specialist in another discipline. Take advantage!

- Reduce group size or add an additional staff person to achieve an increased staff-to-child ratio. Either option creates a better program environment for all children and allows for individual attention when necessary.

- Assess the physical arrangement of the program area and ways the space could better meet the needs of all the children. Would a different location provide easier accessibility or have better lighting conditions? Could the space and surroundings be modified to reduce distractions and create a more "enclosed" environment for a very active, easily distracted child? Is there room for special equipment, chairs, or positioning devices needed by a child with a physical disability?

- Encourage socialization by having children pair up and assist each other. Give children specific roles that will facilitate the situation (e.g., Johnny can sit next to Jim and hold the book for both of them, or Susie can do the cutting and Kathy can do the folding).

- Encourage socialization between disabled and nondisabled peers by providing "props" that encourage role play, communication, and joint play such as dolls, puppets, hats, dress-up clothes, cars and trucks, kitchen sets, and so forth.

- Promote and facilitate play by arranging toys in a variety of ways to help children get started. Initiate a block construction so children have a model to follow, group dolls together with some doll furniture, or place farm animals inside an enclosure of blocks. Helping children make the mental connections that promote play is a simple adaptation for a child whose developmental disabilities may need a little intervention.

- Purchase equipment that accommodates special needs and makes it easier for parents to bring their children to the library. This might include an adjustable chair (possibly with a tray attachment), foam rolls and wedges, or even an assortment of pillows or a beanbag chair to assist with positioning. Wedges and rolls are great fun for infants and toddlers and can be used in a variety of ways by many children.

- Recognize that children with differing abilities may not have equal physical strength, coordination, or ability to assess risks. Anticipating potential safety hazards is a must.

ADAPTATIONS FOR SPECIFIC TYPES OF DISABILITIES

Adaptations vary based on the individual needs of the child and the particular disability. Some disabilities may require further adaptations than the ones listed in the guidelines above.

VISUAL IMPAIRMENTS

Children with visual impairments can easily become isolated. Those with severely limited vision, unable to watch and observe other young children at play and to learn through imitation and modeling, need opportunities for hands-on exploration and exposure to materials that stimulate all of their senses. Sometimes one-on-one guidance in developing new skills is necessary. Keep in mind that total blindness is relatively rare and that most visually impaired children have some degree of vision.

To include a visually impaired child in a group program, be sure to orient the child to the surroundings and the location of staff. Staff should introduce themselves and either introduce the children or have them call out their own names. In a one-on-one situation, gently place a hand on the child's shoulder to gain his attention and/or address him by name. Older children who visit or attend library programs unaccompanied by their parents should be oriented to the children's room, the location of large pieces of furniture, the bathrooms, and so forth.

Do not do for the child what he can do for himself. Encourage independence by teaching or demonstrating the desired activity, hand-over-hand if necessary. Assume competence even if progress is imperfect or slow (a developmentally appropriate approach for all children learning new skills). If parents are participating, have the parent guide the child through the finger play or art activity. This is the time when an extra staff person is very helpful.

Remember that sudden or unexpected movements and unfamiliar textures and sounds may be frightening, especially for younger children.

Choose books for storytime that encourage oral participation ("call and repeat" refrains) and in which the language carries the story and illustrations are of secondary importance. Embellish stories with animated voices, sound effects, and verbal descriptions to aid the visualization of things that may not be apparent or familiar to the visually impaired child.

Use big books and oversized flannel board pieces in bright colors that contrast distinctly from the background color.

Incorporate music, songs, and rhythm instruments into storytimes. Substitute clapping or foot stomping for silent hand movements in participatory songs and finger plays.

Provide thematic "props" (stuffed animals, dolls, puppets, physical items/realia) to augment the story for the child, supplementing aural learning with a tactile experience.

Incorporate games that use senses other than sight. Emphasize hearing, touching, and smelling.

In toy-based programs provide materials that stimulate or rely on senses other than visual (e.g., musical instruments, push toys with noise accompaniment, toys that talk, activity centers that respond with sound effects, and toys that depend on tactile senses like puzzles, shape sorters, pegboards, and pop beads). Consider creating texture boards or using tubs of tactile-rich materials like oatmeal, rice, or commercially available sand/water tables.

Increase tactile stimulation by adding sand to fingerpaint or Velcro to block surfaces. Provide opportunities to play with clay or play dough. Include a variety of textures in gluing activities by incorporating cloth, sandpaper, corrugated cardboard, and twigs with traditional construction paper. Some children may be reluctant to touch unfamiliar materials (tactile defensiveness). Make texturally rich materials available but never force the situation. Describe the texture to enrich language and provide information to the children about a new experience for which they have no visual cues to prepare them. Try substituting a different texture (dry instead of wet, smooth or soft instead of rough) that may be more pleasing.

Increase visual contrast to aid a child in distinguishing between the table and the drawing paper. Add color paint to glue so a child can distinguish from the paper or outline the areas where the puzzle pieces fit to emphasize the shape.

Provide a box top or similar item to define the borders of an activity and keep objects from straying.

Give simple directions to help children interact more appropriately with each other (e.g., "Let's roll, not throw, the ball to Jenny and tell her when we're going to roll it in her direction").

Describe activities and provide verbal information to the visually impaired child, giving advance warning about transitions. Don't avoid words like "see" and "look."

Create smaller, more contained areas for infants to explore freely and safely with barriers made from pillows or empty boxes.

Purchase braille or tactile versions of popular games like checkers. Adapt game pieces with Velcro, heavy-duty tape, or Hi-Marks (a tube-dispensed plastic product that dries to create raised borders, dots, lines, etc.). Adapted games allow sighted and nonsighted children to play together.

Consider labels and signs in braille, raised and/or large print with high contrast colors (at child-height).

Be prepared to provide personal assistance in locating and retrieving library materials. Have a supply of tactile and sniff 'n' smell books, recorded children's books on audiocassette, and braille and large-print books for in-library use and circulation. Consider the purchase of some special equipment for the library such as a Kurzweil reader, a large-print computer screen, or a voice synthesizer for computers. Use a photocopy machine to enlarge text and have magnifying devices available.

MENTAL AND COGNITIVE DISABILITIES

Children with mental and cognitive disabilities may be slower in several developmental areas, including motor coordination, hand/eye coordination, speech and language development, and cognitive development. They may be very friendly or withdrawn, impulsive or excessively timid, easily overstimulated or difficult to engage. Oblivious to social cues from other children, they may get frustrated if their displays of affection are spurned. Interacting with children their own age stimulates social development and provides models of appropriate behavior.

During storytimes, select books with clear, uncomplicated illustrations and stories representing experiences and objects familiar to young children (photographic illustrations work well). Enhance with flannel boards, realia, and puppets. Use rhyming books and books calling for participation and repetitive responses. Reading stories with flair and emphasis, diverting slightly to provide explanations, helps children focus their attention. Clarifying what may be unclear can help the cognitively impaired child stay with the story and may also be helpful for others in the group with limited attention spans.

Choose activities that stimulate several senses at once and provide lots of hands-on opportunities and multisensory stimulation. Offer choices that are simple and clear, limiting alternatives to two.

Keep directions simple. Break down activities into small steps, demonstrating each step and providing one-on-one support if necessary. Reinforce each step with praise and encouragement.

Keep in mind that some children may require more assistance and guidance to participate. Consider having an extra staff person or parent in the room.

Anticipate that transitions—free play to circle time; active finger plays and singing to quiet story—may be difficult for the child. Keep program routines consistent, using repetitive cues, songs, or directions to ease transitions from one activity to another.

Be very safety conscious. Children may not anticipate dangers and adverse consequences.

Be prepared to restructure the environment, or help parents to do so, in order to create a more self-contained, less stimulating corner or area for overly active children to explore. They can gradually expand their exploration when they are ready.

Initiate activities with a child who is passive. Shy and withdrawn infants and very young children may need a great deal of gentle stimulation and coaxing to respond. Their parents may also need extra encouragement and support from library staff as they try to elicit eye contact or a smile. Keep in mind that children often perform better with other children. Try pairing children to encourage participation in activities.

GROSS/FINE MOTOR IMPAIRMENTS

Children with motor impairments do not have full use of their bodies. If they have gross motor impairments, the child may suffer from paralysis of the legs, deformities of the spine, abnormal muscle tone, or other central nervous system injuries, all of which interfere with the child's ability to walk, jump, and play. They may need to use a prosthesis, a wheelchair, crutches, standing boards, or other equipment to help them participate in activities.

If motion activities are called for in a song or circle time activity, initiate activities *all* the children can do. For example, substitute blowing or some other action in place of clapping, or arm and hand movements in place of standing.

Keep pillows, bean bag chairs, or bolsters available to use as positioning aids. Consider purchasing a special chair that can help children who need extra support or special positioning to participate in library programs.

Be sure materials are accessible and within reach of children in wheelchairs. They need opportunities to independently explore the environment.

In play programs, provide tunnels, cushioned ramps and rolls, or large balls to encourage movement and exploration. Include aids that all children will enjoy using, regardless of motor limitations.

Make sure seating arrangements for programs do not isolate any child.

Children with fine motor impairments have limited use of their arms, hands, and fingers. They will experience difficulties in grasping objects, holding pencils or crayons, copying lines and circles, using feeding utensils, and manipulating clothing fasteners. Make things easier to grasp by using beads or spools attached with glue, screws, or tape to puzzle pieces, cookie cutters and other items the child may need to manipulate. Have available large pencils, crayons, and easy-to-use scissors, or adapt ordinary utensils by using tape to thicken the handle of a paintbrush or pencil.

Provide particular toys for children with fine motor impairments including magnetic or bristle blocks, large knobbed puzzles, toys designed to interact with commercially available or homemade adaptive switches, or toys that respond to voice or sound commands. Attach Velcro to ordinary stacking blocks and have some dolls whose clothes fasten with Velcro as well as the more difficult buttons and snaps.

Provide adaptive equipment for computers such as touch screens or a track ball rather than a mouse.

LEARNING DISABILITIES/EMOTIONAL AND ATTENTION DISORDERS AND OTHER "HIDDEN DISABILITIES"

Children with learning disabilities, attention disorders, or other "hidden disabilities" often exhibit behavior that seems inappropriate for their age. Those with attention disorders may be very active, easily distracted, inattentive, disruptive, and impulsive. They may have difficulty following directions. Others become easily frustrated when their disability makes it difficult for them to learn as quickly or in the same way as their peers. These children often draw a great deal of negative attention from staff, other parents, and children.

Awareness training is particularly helpful in sensitizing staff to the possibility of hidden disabilities. It can promote a nonjudgmental attitude and teach specific strategies that will help make the child's library experience successful. Chapter 5 provides information on issues of staff sensitivity and awareness. It is important to know that medically certifiable learning disabilities qualify a child for resources available through the National Library Service for the Blind and Physically Handicapped.

Because there may be no visible manifestations, librarians need to consider the possibility that a learning disability may be contributing to a child's frustration and/or inappropriate behavior. These disabilities may be the most difficult for which to adapt. The librarian may be unaware that a disability exists unless the parent chooses to share such information. In any case, when working with children with attention or learning disorders, it helps to keep the following general guidelines in mind:

> Find ways to engage the child and redirect his energies. During storytime, ask the child to help turn the pages of the book. Have him hold a stuffed animal or puppet associated with the story as a physical "anchor," helping him to focus his attention.

Acknowledge success when the child participates in programs or behaves properly in the library. Offer frequent, positive verbal praise to reinforce appropriate behavior. Explain clearly what to do instead of what *not* to do.

Help these children make the connection between negative behavior and its consequences. Children may not understand how their pushing or grabbing causes other children to withdraw from them. Rather than just saying "Stop" or "Don't do that," explain how the other children feel. Be prepared to intervene if necessary or encourage the parent to do so by using calm but firm language, maintaining eye contact and reinforcing with a gentle hand on the shoulder to focus attention.

Be prepared to alter the environment in the program room or in the children's area to create a quieter, less stimulating, more contained space for the child to play in and explore. Capitalize on corner spaces and use chairs, large blocks, low shelving, or pillows to create smaller spaces. Put up "roadblocks" using large chairs or a table to inhibit running in an area that is usually wide open. Consider softening the lights during storytime to set a quieter, less stimulating tone.

Encourage parents to arrive early for a program to allow the child to become acclimated to the environment. Make sure there are enough materials for all the children, with duplicates of the most popular items to discourage grabbing and squabbling. Provide limited choices to avoid overstimulation.

Prepare children for transitions in activities by verbally explaining what is coming next and using signals to indicate a change of activity (flash lights, use a consistent piece of music, song, or circle game, etc.).

For children with limited attention spans, help them extend their program participation through the next story or song. Arrange ahead with the parent to remove a child once he's reached his limit, working toward extending that limit on the next visit.

If there are consistently quieter, less crowded times in the children's room, suggest to parents that they may find this a better alternative for their library visit. Introduce options for more calming, less active activities such as the use of earphones when listening to an audiocassette with an accompanying book.

With school-age children, be specific and brief with directions, and clear and consistent about rules and expected behavior. Assume that the child will comply but have a "time-out" procedure worked out in advance with the parent if behavior exceeds what can be accommodated in a group setting.

For children with reading disabilities, provide information resources in alternative formats (recorded books, storybook/cassette combos, videotapes, computer CDs, and educational software). Encourage parents to enroll their child in library storytimes and to read aloud regularly at home, providing lots of aural reading experiences. Even if the technical process of reading or learning to read is challenging, parents and librarians need to provide many opportunities that nurture a love of literature and the language enrichment provided by stories.

HEARING IMPAIRMENTS

A child with a hearing impairment may be difficult to identify unless a hearing device is visible or the child's speech or pitch of voice draws attention. Language skills may be very limited, especially in young children. In general, remember that carpeted floors help to absorb distracting background noise and that good lighting is important to those depending on visual cues (sign language, lip reading, or facial expression) to aid their communication.

When addressing the child who is hard of hearing, always speak directly to the child, not to the parent or interpreter. Approach the child on her level, getting the child's attention through eye contact or a gentle touch. Use facial expressions and gestures to aid communication. Demonstrate for other children how they can get the child's attention by a gentle touch on the arm.

Be prepared to engage the services of a sign language interpreter for storytimes and other children's programs if the child is fluent in sign language and having an interpreter would make the program accessible to the child. This pertains to the parent who is deaf as well if the program is geared for the parent and child together. Check local schools for the deaf or local colleges that offer sign language classes for referrals to sign language interpreters. If funds are a problem, perhaps an advanced student could use the experience for class credit. If children are receiving services through early intervention or their local school district, a sign language interpreter for library-based programs may be provided as part of the child's IFSP or IEP.

Observe the child closely for gestures, signs, and eye movements that indicate attempts at communication. Encourage and reinforce these efforts.

Position the child directly in front of the presenter during programs. Position the interpreter near the librarian holding the picture book so that the child can follow the activity more easily. Place flannel boards or other visuals between the librarian and the interpreter.

The area should be well lit, with the staff and interpreter facing into the light. Avoid positioning the presenter or sign language interpreter with their backs toward a window, eliminating glare that makes it difficult for the child to see clearly.

Use activities that rely on other senses. Finger plays, with their descriptive hand and body motions, and touching and smelling games are particularly suitable for children with hearing impairments. If the child is willing, have him or her share some simple signs with the other children. This provides a wonderful opportunity for all the children and a special chance to shine for the child with a hearing impairment.

Programs that are primarily visual such as puppet plays, magic shows, craft demonstrations, hands-on art activities, and captioned movies work well for children who are deaf or hard of hearing.

Picture boards with visual depictions of commonly asked questions and directions may aid communication, particularly with school-age children. Be prepared to demonstrate craft activities, step by step, and repeat if necessary.

Consider installing special equipment in the programming room which, when used in conjunction with an amplifier, enhances sound for those with hearing impairments.

Encourage staff to become familiar with and take instruction in sign language. Perhaps classes can be made available in the library.

SPEECH/LANGUAGE DELAYED/COMMUNICATION DISORDERS

Children with speech or communication disorders may have difficulties with one or a combination of the following: auditory comprehension (they do not understand what is being said to them); expressive communication (they do not possess the vocabulary to converse, state their needs, or label objects); articulation (their speech lacks intelligibility because words are pronounced incorrectly); or a structural defect (a deformity of the mouth, palate, or throat that makes language difficult to understand, such as a cleft palate). They may appear to be disinterested or distracted and can get easily frustrated if they do not get their needs met through communicating.

During programs, use books with interactive, call-and-response activities; objects to be identified; and refrains that encourage children to join in and repeat.

Do not pressure a child to talk but initiate conversation and respond to all of the child's attempts at communication. Repeat and expand on these attempts as part of the conversational give-and-take.

Describe your actions out loud as you do them, naming objects, giving visual cues, asking questions, and, in general, modeling and prompting communication whenever possible.

Make play activities available that encourage verbal interaction among children and stimulate language, such as dolls, puppets, dress-up clothes, blocks, a kitchen area, and a sand/water table.

EXAMPLES OF LIBRARY ADAPTATIONS: LIBRARY STORIES

LIBRARY ADAPTATION #1: SPACE ARRANGEMENTS

Mrs. R. came to visit the library with three-year-old Carlos and her two-year-old twins. All three children were receiving early intervention services. Carlos was particularly impulsive, active, and easily distracted. With all three together, Mrs. R. found it impossible to look for books or have them play in the library's early childhood area. While she ran to keep the three year old from running into the elevator, the twins were wreaking havoc with the board books. The situation was unpleasant for the parent, the children, and the library staff.

The librarian spoke with Mrs. R., acknowledging how difficult the situation was, and suggested the possibility of bringing along another adult or bringing the children separately so they could better enjoy their library experience. Neither was an option. The librarian asked if having a gate available to close off one of the entrances to the early childhood area might be helpful. Mrs. R. could position herself with the twins or Carlos near the entry ramp (the second entrance) and the other children would have access to the entire early childhood area. The mother felt this would be manageable and agreed to try.

A staff member donated a no-longer-used Fisher Price gate to the library. Mrs. R. requests that it be put in place when she visits and the staff knows it is available to be used in other similar situations. A simple solution was found to adapt the library environment to meet the needs of this particular family.

LIBRARY ADAPTATION #2: FURNITURE

Billy, a three year old with cerebral palsy, had little muscle tone and was unable to either kneel at the low table or sit in a regular library chair to do the art activity during an early childhood program. The staff consulted with the mother, who recommended a specific chair that would enable her son to sit with the proper support so that he could participate in the art activity. The library purchased the chair, which comes with its own tray but can also be pushed in far enough to the table so that Billy can share the same space as the other children—everyone's preference. Now he uses the chair to participate in many library activities, as do other children with similar needs.

LIBRARY ADAPTATION #3: EQUIPMENT

Sandra is three years old and autistic. She enjoys coming to the library with her mother but becomes easily overwhelmed with the noise and bustle of all the activity in the room. The staff talked with her mom and together they tried various approaches. What has worked best is for the mom to choose a place in the room to sit with Sandra that is toward one of the corners of the room, out of the main traffic. She surrounds Sandra with some of the toys and puzzles she loves. Sandra is able to cope with the general excitement since she has a space of her own.

Her mom also mentioned how much Sandra loves music but she doesn't seem to respond to the tape recorder in the children's room because the overall noise level is such that Sandra gets too distracted. The library supplied a set of plug-in headphones so when Sandra wants to listen to music she has no other competing noises.

For librarians, adapting the environment for young children is a familiar and comfortable strategy, regularly employed in their efforts to provide quality service to families. Additional adaptations may or may not be necessary for those children with special needs. The basic requirements for successful adaptations is communication, observation, and a willingness to solve problems and experiment until the barriers to inclusion are overcome.

RESOURCES

Blakely, Kim, Mary Ann Lang, and Roger Hart. 1991. *Getting in Touch with Play: Creating Play Environments for Children with Visual Impairments*. New York: The Lighthouse.

Blose, Dee A. and Laura L. Smith. 1995. *Thrifty Nifty Stuff for Little Kids: Developmental Play Using Home Resources*. Tucson, Ariz.: Communication Skill Builders.

Chandler, Phyllis A. 1994. *A Place for Me: Including Children with Special Needs in Early Care and Education Settings*. Washington, D.C.: National Association for the Education of Young Children.

Cook, Ruth E., Annette Tessier, and M. Diane Klein. 1995. *Adapting Early Childhood Curricula for Children in Inclusive Settings*. Old Tappan, N.J.: Macmillan.

Crawford, Jackie et al. 1994. *Please Teach All of Me: Multisensory Activities for Preschoolers*. Longmont, Colo.: Sopris West.

Doggett, Libby and Jill George. 1993. *All Kids Count: Child Care and the Americans with Disabilities Act (ADA)*. Arlington, Tex.: The Arc.

Gross, Lois Rubin. 1988. "Handicapped Children in Library Programs." *Colorado Libraries* 14 (June): 29.

Hodge, Staisey. 1995. *Bright Ideas: Caring for Infants and Toddlers with Special Needs*. Little Rock, Ark.: Southern Early Childhood Association.

Learning to Play: Common Concerns for the Visually Impaired Preschool Child. n.d. Los Angeles, Calif.: Blind Children's Center.

The More We Do Together: Adapting the Environment for Children with Disabilities. 1985. New York: World Rehabilitation Fund.

Mulligan, Sarah et al. 1992. *Integrated Child Care: Meeting the Challenge.* Tucson, Ariz.: Communication Skill Builders.

Programming for Serving Children with Special Needs. 1994. Chicago: American Library Association.

Rogovin, Anne and Christine Cataldo. 1983. *What's the Hurry? Developmental Activities for Able and Handicapped Children.* Baltimore: University Park Press.

Story Hour at the Public Library: Ideas for Including Visually Impaired Preschoolers. 1988. Fact sheet produced by the National Library Service for the Blind and Physically Handicapped. Washington, D.C.: The Library of Congress (June).

Walling, Linda Lucas and Marilyn H. Karrenbrock. 1993. *Disabilities, Children and Libraries: Mainstreaming Services in Public Libraries and School Library Media Centers.* Englewood, Colo.: Libraries Unlimited.

Widerstrom, Anne H. 1995. *Achieving Learning Goals through Play.* Tucson, Ariz.: Communication Skill Builders.

PART III: DEVELOPING COLLECTIONS AND SERVICES

9 COLLECTIONS AND MATERIALS FOR YOUNG CHILDREN WITH SPECIAL NEEDS

To fulfill its goal of being the "Preschooler's Door to Learning" and the primary community resource in support of the lifelong learner, the library must provide collections that nurture various styles and modes of learning, respond to individual needs and preferences, and are appropriate for children with a range of developmental abilities. The materials described in this chapter appeal to all young children and are particularly suitable for those with special needs. Though most items are standard fare for libraries, it may be necessary to increase the number and variety of specific items, or circulate a collection previously limited to in-library use. A list of picture books that portray characters with disabilities in inclusive settings is provided, as well as information for ordering materials that are discussed in the chapter.

The old Chinese proverb "I hear and I forget; I see and I remember; I do and I understand" has significance for all ages but particularly for young children. During their concrete stage of development, they learn by doing. Play is their work and toys are their tools. Though toys are appropriate learning materials for young children and critical to fostering emergent literacy, they are not yet regularly found in public libraries. Librarians may have many questions and concerns about initiating a toy collection. The why and how of building a toy collection are thoroughly covered in Chapter 10.

This chapter describes materials (other than toys) that should be included in collections for young children and that lend themselves to meeting the diverse needs of children with disabilities. While many materials can be obtained through regular jobbers, distributors, book stores, and regional libraries for the blind and disabled, suggested ordering sources for specific materials are included. Most companies and organizations provide catalogs and some have Web sites.

While children with disabilities are attracted to the same materials as their peers, they may need to use materials in ways that better suit their individual abilities and modes of learning. There are three basic learning modalities—tactile/kinesthetic, aural, and visual. Though most children learn best through one particular mode, they often use a combination of all three. The same is true for children with disabilities. Except for cases of total blindness or deafness, children with disabilities, while having a preferred mode of learning, will utilize all three modalities to one degree or another.

MULTISENSORY MATERIALS

Sniff 'n' smell books. The scratch-and-sniff activity books, which allow a child to experience a book through the added sense of smell, provide a cause-and-effect reaction that is particularly important for young children with learning and visual disabilities.

Cloth and toy books. Cloth books, designed for the youngest babies, are also useful for preschoolers and kindergartners who lack muscle and eye/hand coordination. The soft fabric of cloth books prevents injury to the child who may drop or throw the book. These books often provide several textures to enhance the tactile/sensory experience for the child. Some cloth books provide skill-building opportunities such as lacing, zipping, snapping, and buttoning activities.

Toy books are often shaped like the subject of the book and sometimes have movable parts (e.g., a book about trucks that is shaped like a truck with movable wheels). Unlike a typical board or picture book, these books provide the child with a concrete interactive object that reinforces the concept or theme of the story. Pop-up books provide a cause-and-effect activity and promote fine motor skill development through manipulation of the illustrations. Pop-ups are extremely popular, but tend to have a short shelf life. For this reason, some libraries limit their use to in-library only. Lift-the-flap books, which provide some of the same stimulation, tend to last longer, are easier to repair and can more easily be included in a circulating collection.

Sources:
ABC School Supply, Inc.
Lakeshore Learning Materials

Puzzles. Many libraries provide in-house or circulating puzzle collections. For children with disabilities, this collection needs to include a variety of large and small knobbed puzzles, large floor puzzles, and those with raised pieces. Keep in mind that the number of pieces does not always correspond to the difficulty of the puzzle.

Sources:
ABC School Supply, Inc.
Childcraft
Kaplan

Lakeshore Learning Materials
Nasco

Puppets, dolls, and flannel board figures. Ideal for developing language skills and encouraging manipulation, these materials encourage socialization, imaginative play, decision making, and problem solving. They provide an emotional outlet for young children. Integrating characters and figures with disabilities promotes acceptance and inclusion. Many of these items are easy to make or can be purchased commercially.
Sources:
ABC School Supply, Inc. (finger, hand, and mitt puppets featuring multicultural, career, animal, and family sets; flannel board materials)
Demco's Kids & Things (plush puppets, dolls, and stuffed animals)
Nancy Renfo Studios (a full line of puppet and adaptive puppetry equipment and materials)
Pediatric Projects (medically oriented materials including dolls and stuffed toys with disabilities—some with removable clothing and disability accessories)

Realia. Young children, especially those with sensory, perceptual, cognitive, and physical disabilities, extend their learning through manipulation of real objects and models. While it may not be practical for public libraries to circulate realia, items such as jungle and farm animals, dolls, etc., can be available for in-house play. Book kits like the Lakeshore Theme Packets, which include the book and miniatures of selected characters and objects from the story, are also stimulating. Be sure to check for small pieces that could present a choking hazard. Most of the sources listed above provide a variety of these items.

CD-ROMs and computer software. CD-ROMs and computer software provide multisensory, interactive learning experiences. Though some products are designed especially for children with disabilities, they can be enjoyed by all young children. As with other materials, use varies with age and the individual child's stage of development and abilities.
Sources:
Creative Communicating
Don Johnston, Inc.
Edmark
Judy Lynn Software
Scantron Quality Computers
Slater Software

Alternative input devices. The standard keyboard, trackball, and mouse are not usable by children with certain disabilities. They also pose a challenge for very young children who lack fine muscle coordination. A variety of alternative input options for computers include touch screens, discover switches, discover boards, draw boards, Intellikeys, and single switches.

Sources:
Don Johnston, Inc.
IBM National Support Center for Persons with Disabilities
Intellitools, Inc.
Mayer-Johnson, Co.
SoftTouch/kidTECH
Technology for Education, Inc.

Online sources. There are many online sources that provide information about disabilities, parenting children with disabilities, and access to support groups. Ability OnLine Support Network (http://www.ablelink.org/): "Putting children and adolescents with disabilities in touch with the world!", is a source that provides children and adolescents with disabilities an opportunity to form friendships, build self-esteem, and share hope and encouragement through e-mail messages. Children as young as five years old participate in this e-mail "penpal" program. Up-to-date information on medical treatments, educational strategies, and employment opportunities is also provided. A more extensive listing of Internet resources for both children and families is provided in Chapter 12.

Equipment. A Kurzweil reader, magnifying devices, a large-print computer screen, a CCTV, a voice synthesizer for computers, a voice-indexed dictionary, a photocopy machine that enlarges, or a braille output device are some of the special equipment that can be purchased or borrowed to assist children with visual disabilities. Often regional library systems, local agencies, or schools can help librarians to locate this equipment for the child.

TACTILE MATERIALS

Books. Recreational reading material for visually impaired children, aged five and older, in braille, recorded, and print/braille format as well as tactile children's books can be accessed through the National Library Service for the Blind and Physically Handicapped Network of cooperating libraries. Produced with raised pictures and textures, tactile books can be felt by a child with a visual impairment or any child who could benefit from the tactile learning mode. A good example is *Roly Goes Exploring: A Book for Blind and Sighted Children, in Braille and Standard Type, with Pictures to Feel as well as to See* by Philip Newth (New York: Philomel Books, 1981). The American Printing House for the Blind is the official source for textbooks in braille, recorded, and large-type format for blind students from preschool through high school.
   Sources:
   American Printing House for the Blind
   National Library Service for the Blind and Physically Handicapped

Twin vision books. Twin vision books combine braille and text. This combination allows both sighted and blind children or adults to share the same book.
   Sources:
   National Braille Press, Inc.
   National Library Service for the Blind and Physically Handicapped
   Seedlings

Materials with raised outlines or textured surfaces. Braille flash cards and typewriters, relief globes and maps, and textured alphabet letters are great learning aids for all young children and invaluable to the child who is visually impaired.
   Sources:
   American Printing House for the Blind

VISUAL MATERIALS

Big books. For children in groups, big books help focus a child's attention and make it easier to see details. They are particularly suitable for children with low vision, learning disabilities, and a variety of cognitive and attention disorders.
Sources:
ABC School Supply, Inc.
Silver-Burdette Ginn (Read Aloud Big Books)

Large-print books. While large-print editions of classics and popular titles exist for older children, they seem to be nonexistent for young children. Many picture, board, and cloth books, however, are printed in larger type. Recommended type size for children with visual impairments ranges from 16 to 18 points. Other recommended features include bold print, large spacing between lines of text, clear uncluttered pages, and a high contrast between the print and the paper. *Now We Can Go* by Ann Jonas (New York: Greenwillow Books, 1986) is one example of a picture book that meets these criteria.

Wordless books. Wordless books are particularly helpful for stimulating oral communication. They range in sophistication from those with very simple storylines and clear, large pictures to complicated plots and very detailed, intricate pictures. It is important to match the book with the child's physical and cognitive abilities.

Books with text and sign language. "Signed" books illustrate the motion of the signs in conjunction with the text. Using signed books helps hearing and hard-of-hearing adults and children learn sign language and share books together. There are two types of sign language: American Sign Language (ASL) and Signed English. While a library needs to provide some materials in both formats, knowledge of local preferences may influence the type and size of the collection.
Sources:
Gallaudet University Press and Gallaudet University Book Store

Captioned videos. For children with learning disabilities, videos are often a preferred format because they provide entertainment and information and the children don't have to struggle with print. For those with hearing impairments there are both closed-captioned (requiring a decoder) and open-captioned (sign or text appears on the screen) videos. Many popular videos are already available in closed-captioned or open-captioned format.

Sources:
Gallaudet Book Store and Press
Sign Media Inc. (American Sign Language, instructional and entertainment videos)

CD-ROMs. *Rosie's Walk* is an example of a popular story in a sign language CD-ROM format. Created by the Texas School for the Deaf, it is available in both ASL and Signed English.

AURAL MATERIALS

Talking books/recorded books. Talking books are particularly necessary for those who have difficulty physically holding a book, seeing pictures or print, or have learning disabilities that require reinforcement through a variety of learning modes. These types of books on tape are available through the National Library Service for the Blind and Physically Handicapped, an agency that serves all residents of the United States who have a temporary or permanent disability that prevents them from using conventional books. They also provide the special tape machines, required for use of talking books, free of charge.

Audiocassettes of popular books for children of all ages are readily available and are ideal for all children as well as children with visual impairments. They are available through regular library suppliers and local distributers and book stores.

Videos with voice-over narration. In addition to the regular soundtrack, these videos provide voice-over narration that describes in detail what is visually happening on the screen.
Sources:
Bert Hecht
DVS

RESOURCES THAT SUPPORT AND PROMOTE INCLUSION

In addition to collections targeted to children with special needs, it is important for libraries to provide access to materials that portray children with disabilities in inclusive settings. The early childhood years are the time when individuals develop a sense of trust and acceptance. Young children need to have exposure to stories and pictures that include children with disabilities. Sharing common experiences in inclusive settings helps children accept individual differences. Materials that emphasize similarities and shared interests rather than differences build self-esteem of children with disabilities and promote inclusion among their peers.

BOOKS TO SHARE WITH YOUNG CHILDREN

Amenta, Charles A. 1992. *Russell Is Extra Special: A Book about Autism for Children.* New York: Magination Press.

Arnold, Katrin. 1982. *Anna Joins In.* Nashville, Tenn.: Abingdon Press.

Brown, Tricia and Fran Ortiz. 1984. *Someone Special, Just Like You.* New York: Holt, Rinehart, and Winston.

Bunnett, Rochelle. 1995. *Friends at School.* New York: Star Bright Books.

———. *Friends in the Park.* 1992. New York: Checkerboard Press.

Caseley, Judith. 1991. *Harry and Willy and Carrothead.* New York: Greenwillow Books.

Cohen, Miriam. 1983. *See You Tomorrow, Charles.* New York: Greenwillow Books.

Dwight, Laura. 1992. *We Can Do It!* New York: Checkerboard Press.

Fassler, Joan. 1975. *Howie Helps Himself.* Chicago: Albert Whitman and Company.

Greenberg, Judith E. 1985. *What Is the Sign for Friend?* New York: Franklin Watts.

Greenfield, Eloise. 1980. *Darlene.* New York: Methuen.

Holcomb, Nan. *Andy Opens Wide; Cookie; Danny and the Merry-Go-Round; Fair and Square; How About a Hug; Patrick and Emma Lou; Sarah's Surprise; A Smile from Andy* (and other titles in the Turtle Books Series). Hollidaysburg, Pa.: Jason and Nordic Publishers. (NOTE: A workbook, entitled *Sensitivity and Awareness: A Guide for Developing Understanding among Children,* is also available from the publishers for parents and professionals to use in conjunction with the Turtle Books Series.)

Kaufman, Curt and Gita Kaufman. 1985. *Rajesh.* New York: Atheneum.

Kraus, Robert. 1971. *Leo the Late Bloomer.* New York: Windmill Books.

Lasker, Joe. 1980. *Nick Joins In.* Chicago: Albert Whitman and Company.

Levi, Dorothy Hoffman. 1989. *A Very Special Friend.* Washington, D.C.: Kendall Green.

Litchfield, Ada B. 1976. *A Button in Her Ear*. Chicago: Albert Whitman and Company.

McMahon, Patricia. 1995. *Listen for the Bus: David's Story*. Honesdale, Pa.: Boyds Mills Press.

Moss, Deborah M. 1989. *Lee, the Rabbit with Epilepsy* and *Shelley, the Hyperactive Turtle*. Kensington, Md.: Woodbine House.

Osofsky, Audrey. 1992. *My Buddy*. New York: Henry Holt.

Quinsey, Mary Beth. 1986. *Why Does That Man Have Such a Big Nose?* Seattle: Parenting Press.

Rabe, Berniece. 1988. *Where's Chimpy?* Niles, Ill.: Albert Whitman and Company.

Rosenberg, Maxine B. 1983. *My Friend Leslie: The Story of a Handicapped Child*. New York: Lothrop, Lee and Shepard Books.

Russo, Marisabina. 1992. *Alex Is My Friend*. New York: Greenwillow Books.

Schwier, Karin Melberg. 1992. *Keith Edward's Different Day*. San Luis Obispo, Calif.: Impact.

Snell, Nigel. 1979. *Peter Gets a Hearing Aid*. London: Hamish Hamilton.

Stefanik, Alfred. 1982. *Copycat Sam: Developing Ties with a Special Child*. New York: Human Sciences Press.

Thompson, Mary. 1992. *My Brother Matthew*. Rockville, Md.: Woodbine House.

Walker, Lou Ann. 1985. *Amy: The Story of a Deaf Child*. New York: Lodestar Books.

Watson, Esther. 1996. *Talking To Angels*. New York: Harcourt Brace and Company.

OTHER RESOURCES

Mister Rogers' Neighborhood, the award-winning public television program, regularly features children with disabilities as part of the neighborhood. Its parent company, Family Communications, publishes "Around the Neighborhood," a newsletter that offers a calendar showing the themes and dates for each program with follow-up activities. Their catalog includes *Mister Rogers* videos, many of which integrate children with disabilities and related themes in daily experiences.

Kids on the Block produces puppet shows appropriate for young children featuring characters with various disabilities. They perform at libraries, schools, and other community places. To find the Kids on the Block program nearest to the library, contact Kids on the Block.

Friends Together: More Alike than Different, a poster set available from Checkerboard Press, includes 12 color posters depicting children with and without disabilities involved in various activities. The back of each poster describes inclusive early childhood activities appropriate to use with young children.

Sources:
Checkerboard Press

Family Communications
Kids on the Block
Woodbine House

For a more extensive listing of materials for specific disabilities, consult *Disabilities, Children, and Libraries: Mainstreaming Services in Public Libraries and School Library Media Centers* by Linda Lucas Walling and Marilyn H. Karrenbrock (Englewood, Colo.: Libraries Unlimited, 1993). Suggestions for a core collection of materials for very young children can be found in *Running a Parent/Child Workshop: A How-To-Do-It Manual for Librarians* by Sandra Feinberg and Kathleen Deerr (New York: Neal-Schuman, 1995). *Computer Resources for People with Disabilities: A Guide to Exploring Today's Assistive Technology* by the Alliance for Technology Access (Alameda, Calif.: Hunter House, 1994) offers a comprehensive overview of available technology. Local schools serving young children with disabilities are very often willing to share information and expertise on various resources and ways to best utilize materials with young children.

ORDERING SOURCES

ABC School Supply, Inc.
3312 N. Berkeley Lake Road
P.O. Box 100019
Duluth, GA 30136–9419
(800) 669–4222

American Printing House for the Blind
P.O. Box 6985
Louisville, KY 40206–0085
www.aph.org/

Bert Hecht
Audio Optics, Inc.
Hutton Avenue #26
West Orange, NJ 07052

Checkerboard Press
30 Vesey Street
New York, NY 10007
(212) 571–6300

Childcraft
P.O. Box 29149
Mission, KS 66201–9149
(800) 631–5652

Creative Communicating
P.O. Box 3358
Park City, UT 84060
(801) 645–7737

Demco's Kids & Things
P.O. Box 7488
Madison, WI 53707–7488

Don Johnston, Inc.
1000N Fand Road, Bldg.115
P.O. Box 639
Wauconda, IL 60084–0639
(800) 999–4660

DVS
P.O. Box 555742
Indianapolis, IN 46205
(317) 579–0439

Edmark
P.O. Box 97021
Redmond, WA 98073–9721
(800) 362–2890
E-Mail—edmarkteam@edmark.com
www.edmark.com

Family Communications
4802 Fifth Avenue
Pittsburgh, PA 15213
(412) 687–2990

Gallaudet University Press and Gallaudet University Book Store
Gallaudet University
800 Florida Avenue, NE
Washington, DC 20002–3695
(800) 621–2736
(888) 630–9347 (TTY)

IBM National Support Center for Persons with Disabilities
P.O. Box 2150
Atlanta, GA 30301
(404) 988–2733
(800) 462–2133

Intellitools, Inc.
55 Leveroni Court, Suite 9
Novato, CA 94949
(800) 899–6687

Judy Lynn Software
P.O. Box 373
East Brunswick, NJ 08816
(908) 390–8845
www.castle.net/~judylynn

Kaplan
P.O. Box 609
Lewisville, NC 27023–0609
(800) 334–2014

Kids on the Block
9385 Gerwig Lane
Columbia, MD 21046
(800) 368–KIDS

Lakeshore Learning Materials
2695 E. Dominguez Street
P.O. Box 6261
Carson, CA 90749
(800) 421–5354

Mayer-Johnson, Co.
P.O. Box 1579
Solana Beach, CA 92075–7579
(619) 550–0084
E-mail—mayerj@aol.com
www.mayer-johnson.com

Nancy Renfo Studios
P.O. Box 164226
Austin, TX 78716

Nasco
901 Janesville Avenue
P.O. Box 901
Fort Atkinson, WI 53538–0901
(800) 558–9595

National Braille Press, Inc.
88 Saint Stephen Street
Boston, MA 02115
(617) 266–6160

National Library Service for the Blind and Physically Handicapped
Library of Congress
Washington, DC 20542
http://lcweb.loc.gov/nls/nls.html

Pediatric Projects
P.O. Box 1880
Santa Monica, CA 90406–1880

Scantron Quality Computers
20200 Nine Mile Road
St. Clair Shores, MI 48080
(800) 777–3642
E-Mail—sales@sqc.com
www.sqc.com

Seedlings
P.O. Box 2395
Livonia, MI 48151–0395
(800) 777–8552

Sign Media Inc.
4020 Blackburn Lane
Burtonsville, MD 20866

Silver-Burdette Ginn
299 Jefferson Road
Parsippany, NJ 07054
(973) 739–8000
www.esu3.k12.ne.us/support/sbg.html

Slater Software
351 Badger Lane
Guffey, CO 80820
(719) 479–2255
http://home.earthlink.net/~jimslater

SoftTouch/kidTECH
3182 Pinewood Lake Drive
Bakersfield, CA 93309
(805) 396–8676

Technology for Education, Inc.
2300 Lexington Avenue South, #202
St. Paul, MN 55120
(800) 370–0047
E-mail—tfe@pop3.spacestar.com

Woodbine House
6510 Bells Mill Road
Bethesda, MD 20817
(800) 843–7323

10 PLAYING AND LEARNING: IMPLEMENTING A TOY-LENDING SERVICE

It is easy to dismiss the importance of play for young children. In a culture based on an orientation towards "work," the play activities and toys of children often are seen by adults as frivolous and entertaining, not as intrinsically valuable. Nothing could be further from the truth. Research studies have demonstrated repeatedly that children develop their physical, mental, sensory, social, and other learning skills through play.

The lack of availability of appropriate toys creates obstacles to learning through play for children with disabilities. Establishing a toy-lending collection at the library not only provides appropriate toys for use at home, but encourages families to appreciate the central importance of play in a young child's development. A toy collection that integrates commercial toys—and ideas for adapting them—with specially designed adaptive toys entices families and children with a wide range of disabilities to come to the library and utilize its resources.

Providing a toy collection tells all families with young children that libraries are fun and welcoming places. For a child with a significant disability that limits his or her ability to move or communicate or manipulate a toy, however, the availability of toys is more than delightful. It can make the difference between whether or not the child can independently experience the pleasure and learning afforded by play.

TOYS, PLAY, AND LITERACY

Before embarking on developing a toy-lending collection, it is important to examine the rationale for this type of service. The National Lekotek Center, a leader in the development of toy-lending libraries, was founded on the principle of play and the use of toys to promote literacy in children with disabilities. Roughly translated from Swedish, Lekotek means "play library." The Lekotek concept originated in Sweden in 1963 when two mothers of children with disabilities began to seek ways to help their children during their early formative years. They believed that the first years of life significantly determined later development and that intervention strategies must be a part of a child's earliest experiences. Both women were intimately aware of the loneliness and isolation felt by the family of a child with disabilities. It was important to them to have their children with special needs enjoy as natural a childhood as possible and become part of the mainstream of society. Since the most natural activity of young children is play, a play-based approach to the inclusion of children with disabilities became the guiding philosophy of the Lekotek movement.

Children's play sets the foundation for the emergence of literacy. Recently, researchers found that play experiences and supportive parent-child interactions (as well as access to books, print materials, and writing tools), are critical for the emergence of reading and writing skills in young children (Snow et al., 1991; Spodek and Saracho, 1993). Literacy is a dynamic, lifelong, developmental process in which the individual's abilities, relationships with others, and environmental opportunities interact.

This approach to learning holds great promise for children with disabilities because it expands the definition of literacy to encompass a broader range of behaviors. It stresses the importance of a supportive environment, rather than the individual's particular abilities, for learning to read and write. When children with cognitive, physical, communication, or sensory challenges are given access to adapted toys, books, computer equipment, and communication devices, they often have surprised their caregivers and teachers by participating in learning activities—including literacy-building play—that would have been impossible without these accommodations.

If children with disabilities are to develop into readers and writers, they must have the same opportunities to participate in literacy-building play experiences during their early childhood years as their peers without disabilities. Providing these opportunities is the responsibility of libraries dedicated to the development and promotion of literacy. Reaching out in nontraditional ways to children with special needs and providing access to adapted play materials, equipment, and books assures that these children can reach their potential as readers and writers.

To promote inclusion, libraries that circulate toys often include toys for children with and without disabilities. An inclusive collection recognizes the value of toys for all young children and avoids the possibility that children with disabilities will be labeled "special" when they approach the circulation desk. This chapter provides librarians with guidelines and suggestions on developing toy collections not only for children with special needs but applicable for any circulating toy collection.

SELECTION GUIDELINES

Many librarians working with children may not feel they have the education or experience to select toys for children with special needs. The Toy Resource Helpline, operated by the National Lekotek Center, provides free, personalized consultation on how to select appropriate play materials and activities for children with special needs. Lekotek experts have at their fingertips hundreds of resources on where specialized information, equipment, toys, software, and books are available to help families find what they need to promote their children's development and learning. The toll-free help line can be reached by dialing 1–800–366–PLAY.

Local professionals working in the early intervention or special education field can play an important role in toy selection. Many will be happy to share their expertise, especially if the library's collection can be used by their families. Contact them through the local school district, state and local government agencies working in early intervention and special education, or private schools serving children with disabilities. In addition to working with these providers when selecting toys, librarians need to consider the following guidelines.

ADAPTABILITY

A toy collection targeted to children with disabilities needs to include capability switches, specially designed adaptive toys, and generic commercial toys that can be used by children with a range of abilities. These toys and materials promote physical and cognitive growth and empower the child to control his environment.

Capability Switches

Capability switches permit children to activate toys with minimal pressure, sound, or movement. Having a variety of switches available anticipates the needs of individual children and enables them to play with adapted toys. Plate switches of various sizes utilize the slightest pressure from individual body parts whereas other switches may rely on a puff of air or tilt of the head to power the toy. Capability switches include a lighted sensory plate switch, grip switch, vibrating plate switch, joystick, pillow switch, or signal switch.

Adaptive Toys

Adaptive toys are modified, battery-operated toys that can accommodate any capability switch. There are also adaptive toys, such as multisensory activity boxes, bead chains, and stacking towers, that do not require an external switch to be operational. Adaptive toys include toys for sensory play (texture boards, rhythm instruments, etc.);

manipulation toys (tracking boards, lacing sets, etc.); toys that emphasize sensorimotor exploration (multisensory activity boxes, somatosensory bead chains, etc.); toys that stimulate cause-effect or visual tracking (switch-activated toys); and infant sensory stimulation toys (crib mobiles, music box/mirror, floor rollers).

Commercial Toys

Toys need not be specially designed adaptive devices in order to be appropriate for children with special needs. Many generic toys are appropriate for the child with special developmental or physical needs. Choose well-designed toys that are easy to manipulate, are stimulating to multiple senses, show cause and effect, and have potential to be used by children of a wide range of ages and abilities.

The manufacturer-assigned age range for a toy should be interpreted flexibly. A toy geared for a nondisabled three year old may be appropriate for a six year old with special needs. Some features, such as easy-grip puzzle pieces or blocks that connect with magnets or bristles may help make toys more suitable for children with physical disabilities. Adding Velcro can adapt standard building blocks for use with children who lack fine muscle control. Purchasing soft foam instead of hard plastic blocks is safer for all young children. Awareness of safety issues and ways of making toys more accessible is critical. Adaptation guidelines can be found in Chapter 8.

A selection of commercial toys that fall into the following categories should be considered for a core collection:

- building blocks (alphabet blocks, magnetic blocks, bristle blocks, etc.)
- nesting/stacking toys (stacking cups, ring tower, nesting dolls, etc.)
- balls of varying sizes and textures
- dolls and puppets
- easy-grip puzzles
- imaginary play toys (animal sets, dolls, dishes, doctor kits, toy cars and trucks)
- shape/sorting toys
- push/pull toys

VERSATILITY

Just as a library's book collection contains copies of classics, there are certain toys that comprise a core collection. While many families already have basic items in their home collections, certain toys are so important to all children's play—and, therefore, to their development—that no toy collection is complete without them.

In general, these toys exhibit a high degree of "functional versatility" (the ability of a toy to be used in a number of different ways to fit a child's moods, personality, and capabilities). Examples of such toys include balls, dolls, blocks, and stacking/nesting toys. This is in contrast to a toy that can be used only in rigidly defined ways (e.g., jack-in-the-box). Toys that have a high level of functional versatility allow children to use their imagination to fill in the details and expand their use.

While it is not necessary to select only toys with a limited number of pieces, it is important to choose toys that are versatile enough to function even if a few pieces are damaged or lost, such as Duplo blocks or a set of dishes. If each piece of a multiple-item toy is essential to the operation of that toy, it is not an advisable purchase.

QUALITY AND SAFETY

Certain toy companies have established reputations as providers of quality products for children. Be cautious of discount toy catalogs that offer "clones" of popular toys at reduced prices. Products made with inferior materials may not be as durable or safe as their better-known counterparts. For example, one toy discount supplier offers low-priced "easy grip" puzzles, from which the "grip" is easily dislodged from the puzzle piece. This creates a potential choking hazard.

Limit selections to toys that are durable and safe. The better toys are constructed of materials such as shatterproof, durable plastic, safety mirrors, and solid wood rather than flimsy wood laminates. There should be no small pieces that could easily break or fall off.

Bypass toys with hard-to-clean surfaces. Children beyond the toddler years with disabilities may mouth items. Toys that are circulated require a cleaning procedure that is outlined later in this chapter. Selecting toys that have surfaces that can be easily cleaned should be a consideration.

AGE APPROPRIATENESS

At the outset, establish the age level to which the collection is geared. Early childhood includes children from birth to eight years. While it is essential that the age appropriateness of a toy be considered, do not be bound by suggested age levels printed on the package. Many conventional toys geared for younger children may be ideal for older children with special needs.

COST

Parents are less likely to buy some toys because of their cost. This is particularly true for adaptive toys, which are often very expensive. When a library purchases and circulates toys, as with other materials, the cost is a shared expense. The library's toy collection, especially one that includes adaptive toys, gives all children a wider range of choices than any individual family's budget may allow. In addition to sharing expensive resources, the library's toy collection offers an opportunity for parents and children to experience playing with a toy prior to purchasing it.

If the collection includes battery-operated toys, a library must determine whether it can afford to provide batteries on an ongoing basis. Providing batteries can be a costly proposition. One option is to make the families borrowing the toys responsible for providing batteries for their own use. When selecting toys (if the library opts to provide batteries), it is a good idea to keep track of the number and size of batteries each requires, estimate how many times the toy can circulate on one set of batteries, and purchase batteries in bulk. This is a particularly important cost consideration when purchasing adaptive toys and switches, many of which are battery operated.

ORDERING INFORMATION

TOY GUIDES

The National Parent Network on Disabilities partnered with Toys R Us to create *The Toy Guide for Differently Abled Kids!* (Alexandria, Va.: 1997), which focuses on commercially produced toys that have been recommended for use with children with disabilities. In this annually published guide, each toy is described and assigned a symbol that alerts adults to the specific play benefits associated with the toy. The *Guide to Toys for Children Who Are Blind or Visually Impaired* (New York: American Toy Institute) is another valuable guide that is available free from the American Toy Institute.

SOURCES

Some good sources for commercial toys and other materials that might be made available in a circulating collection can be found in Chapter 9. The following are sources for adaptive toys and switches:

Able Net, Inc.
1081 Tenth Avenue SE
Minneapolis, MN 55414–1312
(800) 322–0956

Enabling Devices
385 Warburton Avenue

Hastings-On-Hudson, NY 10706
(914) 478–0906

Flaghouse
150 N. MacQuesten Parkway
Mt. Vernon, NY 10550
(800) 793–7900

Jesana Ltd.
P.O. Box 17
Irvington, NY 10533
(800) 443–4728

Kapable Kids
P.O. Box 250
Bohemia, NY 11716
(800) 356–1564

Switch Kids
8507 Rupp Farm Drive
West Chester, OH 45069–4526
(513) 860–5475

CATALOGING

Toy circulation works best when toys are processed like other collections in the library. When properly cataloged and included in the computerized or card catalog, they are easily accessed by staff and patrons. Guidelines for cataloging toys and other realia can be found in Chapter 10 of *Anglo-American Cataloging Rules* (Chicago: American Library Association, 1988). The Toy Work Form can help librarians to catalog toys in machine readable format (see Figure 11–1).

Figure 11–1. Sample Workform

WFMG	**PUZZLE OR TOY WORKFORM**		

TYPE: r   ELVL: k   SRCE: d   LANG: _ _ _
BLVL: m   TMAT: w   GPUB: _   CTRY: _ _ _
DESC: a   TIME: nnn   DTST: _   DATES: _ _ _ _, _ _ _ _

PHYSICAL
DESCRIPTION   ØØ7   k ‡b z   ‡d _ ‡e_

STOCK
CALL #   Ø37 ♭ ♭

CALL NO.   Ø99 ♭ 9

MAIN ENTRY   1_ _♭

TITLE   245_ _   ‡h toy

          ‡b
          ‡c

IMPRINT   26Ø ♭ ♭   ‡b
          ‡c

PHYSICAL
DESC.   3ØØ ♭ ♭

NOTES   5Ø_ _ _

SUBHEADING   65Ø ♭ Ø   Puzzles
     OR: 65Ø ♭ Ø   Toys
          6_   _ _
          6_   _ _

ADDED ENTRY   7_

CATALOGED BY _____ DATE _____
KEYED BY _____ DATE _____

Many MARC records for toys are available on OCLC. If a specific toy does not yet have a record, librarians can search OCLC for the record of another toy manufactured by the same company. This record provides a template for the toy being cataloged. Checking existing records ensures consistency in the catalog and streamlines accessibility for the user.

PROCESSING

Here are some additional processing tips after a toy has been cataloged:

- Mark each piece of the toy with indelible, nontoxic ink, using an identifying name or number specific to that toy, such as a bar code number.
- Package the toys in bags for storage and circulation. Mesh bags are preferred because they are flexible for use with toys of varying shapes, can be ordered in an assortment of sizes, and are durable and washable. Plastic bags, which are an alternative, cannot be washed and tend to rip more easily or have handles that break after several uses.

Sources for mesh bags:
Academy Broadway Corp.
5 Plant Avenue
Hauppauge, NY 11788
(516) 231–7000
(Nylon Mesh Utility Bag for medium to large toys)

Safety 1st, Inc.
210 Boylston Street
Chestnut Hill, MA 02167
(800) 962–7233
(Wash & Dry mesh bags for small toys)

Attach a laminated identification tag to the mesh bag, using either a nylon or plastic tie. This tag should include the following information: toy title, Dewey decimal number, bar code (or other identifying number), number of pieces, and recommended age range as stated by the manufacturer. Including the recommended age range is helpful in identifying the developmental level for which the toy was designed (see Figure 11–2). If the toy has many pieces, and the loss of a few of them will not keep it from circulating, do *not* include the exact number of pieces on the tag. Instead, substitute a generic description such as "multiple pieces." This will prevent the necessity of producing a new tag each time a piece is lost or destroyed.

Figure 11–2. Sample Tags

CALL NO: TOY COLLECTION J793.7 DOME

TITLE: DOME ALONE WITH SWITCH

CONTENT: 1 SELF-CONTAINED DOME,
                4 C BATTERIES

Place Library Barcode Here

○

THIS ITEM IS NOT RENEWABLE

DO NOT REMOVE THIS TAG

PLEASE CHECK CONTENTS FOR MISSING PIECES.
IF THE TOY IS RETURNED WITH MISSING PIECES,
YOU WILL BE CHARGED FULL PRICE OF TOY.

○

STORAGE

Housing the circulating toy collection out of the public area is advised. Maintaining the collection for circulation purposes is difficult if the toys are left open for public use. Establishing a separate toy collection that includes items such as floor puzzles, puppets, and blocks specifically for children to use in the library setting is recommended.

The storage space needs to be easily accessible to staff members responsible for retrieving the toys. Retrieving toys takes time. Placing it near the children's room yet out of the patron's "reach" is the ideal location.

An efficient and flexible storage system for a toy collection is a wall-grid system, complete with detachable baskets and hooks of various sizes and shapes. Hooks may be used for smaller toys, while larger/heavier toys require the extra support of a basket. This type of storage system provides for collection expansion, since additional grid pieces and accessories may be purchased at a later date. Since this is a wall-mounted system, it can make use of otherwise unusable space, often at a premium in library buildings. Examples of such a space include a basement wall adjacent to an elevator, for easy access by library staff, or the walls of a stairwell directly off the public floor.

Toys may be arranged on the grid by call number, similar to the shelving of traditional library materials. Another option is to arrange the toys according to type (e.g., mazes, puppets, puzzles, manipulative toys, imaginary play, adaptive switches, etc.). A portion of the grid system can be designated for each type, with a color assigned to each section. The same colored label is then affixed to the laminated tag on each toy's mesh bag.

Source for wall-grid system:
Library Display Design Systems
P.O. Box 8143
Berlin, CT 06037
(203) 828–6089

BUDGET

The initial costs for developing a circulating toy collection includes toy purchases, cleaning and storage supplies, publicity materials, and replacement batteries (optional). How and where the toys are housed can also add to the initial budget, depending upon the type of storage units used. Once the toy collection is in place, it becomes less expensive and can be maintained on a smaller budget.

The sample budget (see Figure 11–3) lists the initial costs for the establishment of a circulating toy collection. It does not include staff salaries.

Figure 11–3. Sample Budget

SAMPLE BUDGET

GRID SYSTEM* 15 wall panels (2'x6'), wall mount brackets, grid connectors, baskets, hooks, and freight charges.		$1,450
Optional installation:		$ 370
TOY & CAPABILITY SWITCHES		$2,500
30 adaptive toys + 10 switches	$1,800	
50 commercial toys	$ 700	
PROCESSING, STORAGE, CLEANING SUPPLIES		$ 770
100 mesh bags (assorted sizes)	$ 350	
100 nylon ties (to attach laminated tags to bags)	$ 20	
Assorted batteries for adaptive toys	$ 375	
Cleaning supplies (bleach, cloths spray bottles, markers)	$ 25	
PUBLICITY (brochures, flyers, posters, etc.)		$ 300
TOY BINDERS (2 binders, color copies, plastic inserts)		$ 100

TOTAL ESTIMATED COST (includes installation of grid system)	**$5,490**

* Estimate is for a wall grid system designed to house a much larger collection than the initial number of toys indicated in this budget; this leaves room for expansion or may be down-sized initially to cut costs.

POLICIES AND PROCEDURES

Each toy collection is unique in scope, organization, policies, and procedures. If possible, visit an established toy-lending or play library to observe and learn what works best for them. The USA Toy Library Association, 2530 Crawford Avenue, Suite 111, Evanston, IL 60201, (708) 864–3330 has a complete list of over 300 toy libraries, including facilities for children with special needs.

POLICIES

Here are some of the questions to consider when establishing policies:

- Who can borrow the toys (parents only, each child in the family, grandparents, etc.)?
- How many toys can be borrowed (per family, per child, etc.)?
- What is the length of the loan period?
- Can toys be reserved or renewed?
- What is patron responsibility and liability regarding damaged toys or missing pieces?
- Can out-of-district early intervention professionals borrow items to work with in-district children?

The size of the collection will be a determining factor in many of these policies. If patrons are limited to one toy per cardholder, remember that certain adaptive toys require the loan of a capability switch in order to be activated. Since the toy collection is part of a public library, many lending policies would exclude out-of-district residents from borrowing these items; however, if the size of the collection permits, consideration may be given to early intervention professionals working with families within the library district. Consideration may also be given to local early childhood centers or agencies that would like to borrow toys for use at their site. By expanding the loan of toys to early intervention specialists and agencies, the library reaches children and families that may not be regular library users. Early intervention specialists can assist families in deriving the maximum benefit in the utilization of the toy collection.

PROCEDURES

Necessary to any well-maintained toy collection are clearly stated guidelines regarding access to the toy collection and circulation procedures. Maximizing access with minimal inconvenience to staff and patrons should be of primary importance.

Accessing the Collection

For patrons to use the toy collection, there must be sensible, easy ways for them to discover what toys are in the collection and whether a particular toy is available for circulation. Alternatives include a record in the library card (or online) catalog or a special toy-collection notebook. A record in the computer or card catalog integrates the collection into the library's other holdings. It allows patrons to search for specific toys using standard access points (i.e., subject, toy name, or manufacturer).

A specially designed looseleaf notebook, kept at the children's reference desk, is an alternative method for recording toys. A visual record helps the patron determine whether the toy is appropriate for the child's needs, interests, and abilities. Some libraries keep both the catalog record and a notebook. The notebook contains a one-sheet description of each toy with a picture copied (in color if possible) from the toy catalog or from the box that housed the toy. The description needs to include whether a switch or batteries are required. For durability, this toy record can be laminated or placed in plastic sleeves.

Check-out Procedures

When a patron has chosen a particular toy from either the toy notebook or public access catalog, the staff needs to check the item for availability. Libraries with online catalogs generally have a status entry for each item. If this is not available, other methods may be devised. For example, placing a checked-out card in a pocket attached to the plastic sleeves in the toy notebook alerts the patron that the item is circulating. If the toy is available, a staff member can retrieve the toy for the patron.

Check-in Procedure

When a toy is returned to the library, it is placed in a special bin and not reshelved until a staff member has completed the check-in procedure.

1. Check toy for damage or missing pieces.
2. Clean hard plastic surfaces with a bleach and water solution using a ratio of one tablespoon of bleach to one quart of water (or 1/4 cup of bleach to one gallon of water). This solution must be prepared daily to maintain its effectiveness. A spray bottle is a convenient way to apply the solution. If batteries are stored in the toys, remove the batteries before you clean to prevent corrosion.
3. Replace weak or dead batteries. Keep in mind that batteries stored outside of the toy will have a prolonged life.
4. Check the identification number or bar code on the toy and rewrite the information, if necessary, with an indelible marker. Check that the number matches the bar code on the laminated tag.

5. Check the laminated tag to ensure it is still firmly attached to the bag.
6. Examine the mesh bag and replace if necessary.
7. Reshelve the toy on the wall-grid system.
8. Remove check-out card from notebook, if necessary.

If there are any problems when a toy is returned, an explanatory note or form may be used to describe the problem (e.g., missing tag, ripped bag, lost pieces, or damaged parts). Most toy manufacturers replace parts free of charge or for a nominal fee. An alternative idea is to purchase extra copies of toys to keep for replacement parts.

MARKETING AND PROMOTION

"If you build it, they will come!" is not necessarily true in the case of a new circulating toy collection. Patrons, community agencies, professionals working with families, and the entire library staff must be made aware of this special collection. Remember, toy collections are not typical. The public rarely thinks of accessing toys through the library. In order to promote the toy-lending collection, librarians may adopt specific strategies including publicity, collaboration, and programming.

PUBLICITY

Publicity needs to begin even before the toys are ready to circulate and continue after the collection is developed. Since the toy collection can be beneficial to a wide variety of people (grandparents and others appreciate being able to borrow toys when young children come to visit), publicity needs to target the entire community. Types of publicity include

- in-house flyers and brochures;
- posters;
- press releases in local newspapers;
- personal promotion by library staff;
- displaying toys during library programs.

DISTRIBUTION AND PROGRAMMING THROUGH COLLABORATION

Each community has early intervention agencies that work directly with families and children with special needs. Identifying and working cooperatively with these agencies maximizes the benefits of the toy collection. Flyers publicizing the toy collection can be distributed to early intervention agencies so staff members can utilize the collection and inform their families of its availability.

The librarian can visit these agencies to demonstrate some of the toys to the teachers and explain policies and procedures governing the collection. Special arrangements can be made to circulate these toys to staff members, or a copy of the toy notebook can be kept at the agency for the teachers to refer to. Parent organizations affiliated with the early intervention agencies can be invited to the library for an orientation program.

Special programs can be developed in collaboration with these agencies to promote awareness and demonstrate appropriate ways of using the toys in the collection. Occupational and physical therapists, special education teachers, and other professionals are invaluable facilitators for such programs. Evening programs might be offered to give parents an opportunity to learn how to use the toys or even how to make commercially produced toys adaptable to their children's needs. Special parent/child programs held in the library also give families an opportunity to become familiar with the toys from the collection. The inclusion of early intervention and preschool education providers in such programs provides a personal resource to answer specific questions parents may have on how best to utilize certain toys with their children.

THE LEKOTEK PROGRAM MODEL

In addition to providing toy-lending collections, Lekotek libraries offer programming around the use of toys designed specifically for children with special needs and their families. The underlying principles that Lekotek uses when designing programs serve as guideposts for librarians who wish to offer specialized programming targeted to this audience. Keep in mind that programming offered by a Lekotek library is provided by a trained play leader.

PRINCIPLES AND GUIDELINES
Every child deserves to have fun. Children with disabilities often have extraordinary responsibilities. They must deal with numerous and often painful medical visits, as well as physical and other therapy that focuses on the child working toward outcomes or goals. While the services provided by Lekotek do foster skill development, it is the one visit in the mosaic of services that is designed specifically for fun.

Play should focus on what a child can do, not what he or she can't do. Mastery of skills learned through play with toys and on computers helps to foster feelings of satisfaction and adequacy. Play leaders select toys for children that challenge them to create successes for themselves. The Lekotek approach focuses on identifying each child's skills and competencies and making maximum use of them.

Play sessions are family centered. The entire family system, including parents, siblings, grandparents, and friends, is integral to helping a child with special needs reach his or her potential. All family members are invited to participate in Lekotek play sessions and are encouraged to develop their own style for playing with and supporting the challenged child. The sessions provide opportunities for play leaders to give special attention to siblings, who may sometimes feel overlooked with so much family energy being devoted to the child with the disability. Siblings and young friends are welcome to take home toys from the toy-lending library in hopes that the inclusive patterns of play encouraged at Lekotek are repeated at home.

Play sessions are opportunities to provide family support services. Parents of children with disabilities are often struggling with multiple stresses: caring for a child or children with many needs, paying for high medical costs, managing a schedule that includes frequent health care and therapy visits, advocating for services to which their children may be entitled, and dealing with feelings about parenting a child with disabilities. Play leaders help parents build the set of skills they need to handle this challenging life and to navigate through the maze of information, support systems, and available services.

Play sessions should promote the inclusion of children with disabilities into family and community activities. If children with disabilities are to be included in the play activities of their brothers, sisters, and friends, it's important for them to be able to use the same toys and participate in the same play activities. Play leaders find creative ways to enable children with disabilities to play with the same materials as their nondisabled peers through adapting toys and the ways in which games are played to enable everyone to participate.

FAMILY-CENTERED PLAY SESSIONS
Family play sessions emphasize the creative use and adaptation of toys and play materials for use by children with disabilities, while promoting interactive play among all members of the family. Toys, play materials, books, assistive technology, and software are carefully selected by play leaders to enable as much independent access as possible for the child with special needs.

The selection of play activities and materials incorporates the interests of the child and the child's caregivers and siblings to motivate positive interaction and communication. The Lekotek model draws heavily from research on parent-child interactions, which argues that an important goal of interventions with children with disabilities should be to help support reciprocal and pleasurable interactions between parents and children.

Parents are encouraged to bring brothers and sisters, grandparents, aunts, uncles, cousins, and neighborhood friends to Lekotek play sessions to broaden the circle of support for the child with disabilities. The family spends about an hour playing together with the facilitation of the Lekotek leader. Siblings, in particular, are valued participants in play sessions, since they are the child's most available and natural playmates. Also, siblings of children with disabilities often have less obvious "special needs" themselves, which the Lekotek leader can help the family address. At the end of the play session, the family selects five to eight toys, books, software programs, switches, and other adaptive equipment to use at home until the next play session.

Lekotek play sessions are held either at the library, in the family's home, or at a community location that is convenient for the family. Usually, sessions are held on a monthly basis, but some families may be seen on a weekly basis if the need for more intensive family support services is indicated. Families can choose to participate in individual family sessions or in small-group play sessions. Many Lekoteks also offer inclusive parent-child play groups. In order to be responsive to the needs of families, Lekotek sessions are scheduled in a flexible manner, with evening and Saturday hours offered to enable working parents to attend.

TRAINING FOR PLAY LEADERS

Lekotek play leaders are trained professionals with backgrounds in early childhood, special education, occupational, physical, and speech therapy, or other related fields. They receive additional training from the National Lekotek Center in play facilitation techniques for children with a range of disabilities, toy selection and adaptation, the use of assistive technology, and the provision of family support.

Lekotek play leaders work in close collaboration with other professionals providing services to the children and their families. Play activities and materials are selected to promote the child's relaxed and natural acquisition and practice of skills at home, which have been identified in his Individualized Family Service Plan (IFSP) or Individualized Education Plan (IEP). The focus of Lekotek, however, remains on the child's enjoyment of the play experiences and the family's enjoyment of the child. This approach enables parents to celebrate their child's abilities and participation, without experiencing the pressure to help their child reach specified developmental goals.

Librarians interested in learning more about Lekotek or starting a Lekotek program in their community should contact the National Lekotek Center located in Evanston, Illinois. The National Lekotek Center serves as headquarters for a national network of approximately 50 Lekotek-affiliated toy libraries and computer play programs. Lekotek start-up kits and personalized technical assistance are available to help communities replicate the Lekotek Toy Library model. A special one-week training seminar held at the National Lekotek Center provides the training necessary to start a Lekotek program and begin providing this service to children with disabilities and their families. An additional one-week training seminar, called *Computer Play: Facilitating Inclusion through Technology*, provides specialized training in the use of computers and adapted computer technology for children with disabilities.

Toy collections and play sessions often bring families into the library for the very first time. This is particularly the case for parents and children with disabilities and may very well be the key to changing a family's perception of public libraries. In addition to enabling the young child with a disability to participate in library service and develop literacy skills, toys provide a wonderful opportunity for librarians to attract new patrons and serve as a bridge to other services and programs available for them.

RESOURCES FOR BUILDING A TOY COLLECTION

American Toy Institute. *Guide to Toys for Children Who Are Blind or Visually Impaired*. 200 Fifth Avenue, Suite 740, New York, NY 10010, (800) 851–9955 or (212) 675–1141.

Jackson, Sara. 1992. "A Puff of Breath, a Tilt of the Head and...Presto!...It's a Toy Library for Children with Disabilities." *Mississippi Libraries* 56, no. 3 (Fall): 76–78.

Jackson, Sara. 1996. "Toys, Not Books; A Special Youth Services Program." *Youth Services in Libraries* 9 (Winter): 199–201.

Klauber, Julie. 1996. "Toy Story: How to Select and Buy Adaptive Toys." *School Library Journal* 42, no. 7 (July): 22–25.

National Lekotek Center. *Lekotek Play Guide for Children with Special Needs*; *Play Is a Child's World: A Lekotek Resource Guide on Play for Children with Disabilities for Families, Friends and Professionals*; *Come Play With Me! A Developmental Play Curriculum Guide for Teen Par-*

ents of Children from Birth to Three Years Old; Lekotek Plan Book of Adaptive Toys: Volume I, Volume II, Volume III. 2100 Ridge Avenue, Evanston, IL 60204, (708) 328–0001.

National Parent Network on Disabilities and Toys R Us. 1997. *Toy Guide for Differently Abled Kids: Fifth Edition.* 1727 King Street, Suite 305, Alexandria, VA 22314.

Oppenheim Toy Portfolio. An independent guide to children's media featuring the best in toys, books, videos, and software. Each quarterly issue features a section entitled "Using Ordinary Toys for Kids with Special Needs." 40 East 9th Street, New York, NY 10003, (212) 598–0502.

Schwartz, Sue and Joan Heller Miller. 1996. *The New Language of Toys: Teaching Communications Skills to Children with Special Needs.* Bethesda, Md.: Woodbine Press.

Sinker, Mary. 1986. *Toys for Growing: A Guide to Toys that Develop Skills.* Chicago: Year Book Medical Publishers.

"Switches and Battery Interrupters Made Simple." 1985. *Exceptional Parent* 15 (November): 64–65.

Talcott, Anne E. 1991. "The Early Intervention Resources/Toy Lending Library: Helping 'At Risk' Toddlers and Their Parents." *Ohio Libraries* 4 (Jul/Aug): 8–10.

Walling, Linda Lucas and Marilyn H. Karrenbrock. 1993. *Disabilities, Children, and Libraries: Mainstreaming Services in Public Libraries and School Library Media Centers.* Englewood, Colo.: Libraries Unlimited.

REFERENCES

Snow, Catherine E. et al. 1991. *The Social Prerequisites of Literacy Development: Home and School Experiences of Preschool-Aged Children from Low-Income Families.* Cambridge, Mass.: Harvard Univ.

Spodek, Bernard and Olivia Saracho. 1993. *Language and Literacy in Early Childhood Education*, vol. 4. New York: Teachers College Pr.

PARENT AND PROFESSIONAL RESOURCE CENTERS

Next to the emotional support derived from sharing experiences with other parents of children with disabilities, one of the most critical needs of parents is that for information. In *Guidelines for Establishing a Family Resource Library* (Steele and Willard, 1989, p. 3), the authors identify parents' access to information about their child's health conditions as a key element of the family-centered approach. They cite research upholding the positive relationship between the parents' ability to cope and their understanding of their child's condition. The experience of the New York State's Developmental Disabilities Planning Council (DDPC) and its library-based parent resource centers (see Appendix D) further supports this need and identifies the public library as the logical community location for parents to seek and expect to find information (Lobosco et al., 1996).

WHAT IS A PARENT RESOURCE CENTER?

Parent resource centers go hand-in-hand with inclusive library services for young children. They provide important parenting information to families, promote early identification of developmental needs in children, and help identify community resources available to address these needs. They facilitate information and resource sharing among community agencies regarding parenting and developmental disability issues and provide a range of parenting services to families, caregivers, and professionals in their communities, including

- core collections of resources such as books, videos, magazines, pamphlets, and other educational materials on parenting and child development issues;
- information and referral services connecting patrons to resources and organizations that offer additional information and assistance;
- group educational programs, which range from interactive workshops for parents and toddlers to seminars for adults;
- collaboration with organizations and advocacy groups interested in strengthening parenting resources in their communities;

- outreach activities to engage and serve individuals and community groups who have parent education needs.

This chapter identifies resources and strategies to assist librarians in building library services that meet the needs of parents of children with disabilities and those working to assist them and provides detailed guidelines on developing a parent/professional collection.

PREPARING AHEAD

The development of a typical parent resource center requires time to plan and implement the following strategies

- assigning and hiring staff;
- establishing an advisory committee;
- developing collaborative arrangements;
- preparing space;
- acquiring materials and equipment;
- cataloging materials for circulation;
- developing educational programs;
- building information and referral capacity;
- conducting outreach, public education, and awareness efforts;
- designing initial and ongoing evaluation activities;
- preparing a budget and solidifying ongoing funding.

A model time line for establishing a parent resource center based on the experience of libraries that were involved in the DDPC project (Appendix D) can be found in *Library-Based Parent Resource Centers: A Guide to Implementing Programs* (Cohen and Simkin, 1994).

BUILDING A NETWORK

Early and ongoing collaboration is essential for establishing parent resource centers so that they are responsive to community need. Networks that a library staff builds with service providers, and advocacy and support groups facilitate community awareness and use of library programs. Network members identify and recruit participants who may need parenting information but are not familiar with libraries, assist in resource identification for the parent collection, and sensitize staff to issues such as scheduling, transportation, and child care that may affect program attendance. Additionally, collaboration can result in resource sharing that enables libraries to increase the breadth and quality of the services they offer.

Community input can be gained through focus groups, personal contact with local service provider organizations, or the establishment of a formal advisory committee. Chapters 6 and 7 provide information on working with parents and community resource professionals.

Extensive and detailed information on building collaborations and developing cooperative programs and services can be found in *Serving Families and Children through Partnerships: A How-To-Do-It Manual for Librarians* (Feinberg and Feldman, 1996).

When meeting with key leaders, ask for help in identifying network members, recommending materials for the collection that would be useful to the parents they serve and suggesting speakers for parenting programs and workshops. Potential contacts include

- Association for Retarded Citizens;
- attention deficit disorder support groups and other disability specific organizations;
- Cooperative Extension associations;
- county departments of health and social services and early intervention agencies;
- early childhood direction centers;
- Head Start centers;
- local and regional education agencies;
- maternal and child health clinics;
- mental health associations;
- parent teacher organizations;
- school districts and special preschool programs;
- WIC programs;
- youth bureaus.

PROVIDING REFERENCE, INFORMATION, AND REFERRAL SERVICES

The librarian's skill and sensitivity in helping parents to define the nature and extent of the information they want is critical in order to provide the most useful information without overwhelming the patron. Provide access to appropriate information in a respectful and supportive way, clarifying that a librarian is not a health specialist. Never attempt to assist parents in interpreting medical information. Suggest that they raise specific questions or concerns with their health care provider, hoping that their dialogue can be more useful if the parents are armed with information about the issues. The kind of information they are looking for, their readiness for increasing levels of information, and their ability to absorb this information will probably change over time. Parents need to be the guide for the kind and the extent of the information they require.

Parent resource centers provide information and referral services to connect parents to resources and organizations that offer additional assistance on specific issues. Familiarity with community resources and an ability to organize this information and make it readily available for parents can make a tremendous difference in the lives of families.

Access to these "people" resources and services is a critical piece of the family support collection, augmenting the material resources and elevating the librarian's role as the community information specialist for families.

Whether a card file, book directory, or computer database, the librarian needs to have a mechanism for helping families locate local community resources and services. The library may take the lead in developing and maintaining this file; provide leadership in making this a communitywide, coalition-building process; or simply make available within the library an already existing resource file, directory, or group of directories developed by other organizations. Access to these community resources is critical for all families, and especially families of children with multiple needs. Chapter 6 provides detailed information on how to provide information and referral in the library setting.

As part of the requirement of Part C of the Individuals with Disabilities Act, each state is required to provide a statewide listing or central directory of services for families of children with disabilities. Contact your state department of health or education for information about your state's mechanism for helping families of children with disabilities to locate community resource information. Appendix C provides contact addresses for Part C coordinators.

PROGRAMMING FOR PARENTS AND CAREGIVERS

Parents of children with disabilities often feel a tremendous sense of isolation. Full community involvement in programs at the local library, church, or neighborhood center helps families to connect to one another. Programs can range from the highly interactive Parent/Child Workshop (Feinberg and Deerr, 1995), which offers a wonderful opportunity for parents of children with and without disabilities to participate together in a community setting, to seminars on topics of interest that parents attend individually or in a series. Parents of children with special needs have also noted the importance of parent support groups as forums for developing friendships, establishing mutual sources of respite, and sharing transportation and information. Parent support groups are generally informal gatherings of parents facilitated by its own members. Parents who meet at library-sponsored workshops might choose to develop parent support groups that continue to meet subsequent to the formal program, sometimes in the library and sometimes in participants' homes. *Serving Families and Children through Partnerships: A How-To-Do-It Manual for Librarians* (Feinberg and Feldman, 1996) offers suggestions and guidelines for implementing parent education and support programs in libraries.

PROMOTING AWARENESS AND USE OF THE PARENT RESOURCE CENTER

The community at large needs to be informed of parent resource center collections and services if they are to be well used. Some strategies include

- making formal presentations to community groups;
- distributing bookmarks, flyers, and brochures;
- placing articles and announcements in library newsletters and local newspapers and magazines;
- having informal conversations with community members (in the library and other community locations) to promote the parent programs and services;
- holding an Open House;
- doing radio interviews;
- making announcements through local cable television access;
- asking other organizations such as a local school or special needs preschool program to announce library activities for families in their calendars or post a flyer on a bulletin board.

Generating publicity should be a continuous activity to promote visibility and good feelings about the resource center and the library, as well as lead families to the resource center when they need parenting information. Be sure that publicity reflects the library's commitment to serving all families with young children in the community even if some activities are targeted to specific populations.

LINKING THE LIBRARY'S MISSION TO THE PARENT RESOURCE CENTER

Parent resource centers can advance a library's goals, such as reaching underserved members of the community or responding to the needs of families. If the program is seen as helping the library achieve its goals, it is more likely to obtain the necessary support to initiate and maintain parent collections and activities and to minimize staff resistance to changes in library routines or reallocation of resources. It is particularly important that those individuals who make decisions regarding the ongoing activities of the program understand how the efforts of the parent resource center can influence the library mission. Boards of trustees, Friends of the Library, the library director, and department heads are among those who need to be kept informed on the benefits to the library resulting from the center's activities.

Once the center is under way, it may be necessary to address barriers that emerge and reexamine library policies and practices prompted by staff experiences. Policy changes might include instituting amnesty policies for outstanding library fines that some families are unable to pay or adjusting the number of days that parenting videotapes may be borrowed in order to respond to the needs of parents with limited access to transportation. Critical to the long-term success of a center is the administrative commitment of ongoing resources through either outside funding or internal operating funds.

REACHING OUT TO NEW AUDIENCES

When reaching out to populations that are not regular library users, issues to consider include scheduling programs in the evening or on weekends, providing baby-sitting or programming for siblings, and arranging for transportation (e.g., with vans operated by community groups serving your target audience).

Libraries can benefit from programs organized by outside community groups. Library meeting space for parenting classes may be sought by outside groups because it is free or low cost, centrally located, and considered neutral. Seminars organized by community-based agencies may help the library meet its goals and provide the added benefit of attracting members of the community who are not regular library users. Flexibility and a willingness to become familiar with the culture, needs, and interests of these new constituencies is necessary. It takes time to build awareness and trust and to develop the collaborative relationships with other community agencies that can assist in reaching new audiences. The following are effective strategies:

Identify and enlist the help of "gatekeepers." Gatekeepers are key individuals who can describe the library's programs, introduce them to community members, bring people to the library or cosponsor programs. They may include other parents, staff from a community agency who are trusted by your target audience, respected members of some local support groups, or community leaders such as members of the clergy.

Make personal contact with potential participants. Personal contacts are important for involving new library users. Personal invitations and reminder calls may be needed for new patrons who sign up for workshops and seminars. Once people find that they benefit from using library services and develop comfort at the library, they often bring in others.

Hire staff who already work with or are connected to the target audience. People who are unfamiliar with the library will be more willing to come to programs that involve people they already know. Consider hiring a part-time counselor in a local diagnostic child care program to serve as a part-time bilingual outreach worker for the library; a local Head Start assistant as a part-time library clerk; or special needs child care workers to provide child care at library programs.

Make people feel welcome and anticipate special needs. Conducting programs or displaying collections in ways that are affirming, inclusive, and nonstigmatizing and having equipment and resources that accommodate special needs promote use of collections and services. Anticipating what will make it difficult for people to participate is important. Child care and transportation are two support services frequently identified as critical to promoting use of parent programs. Offering child care or programs for siblings facilitates parent participation in educational workshops. Providing these services through collaboration with other agencies should be explored.

FUNDING

Parent resource centers can be established for as little as $2,000 for a simple streamlined model in which a small collection is purchased for an existing space. Adding additional resources, space, programs, and services adds to the cost. Between $10,000 and $50,000 is needed to initiate a new parent resource center program in a community library. Many libraries can seek outside funding to begin these programs, recognizing that they will ultimately incorporate the project's operating costs into their annual budgets; however, a committed library can establish and maintain a parent resource center without outside funding. Despite some anxiety over funding, it should be noted that all the libraries participating in the New York State Developmental Disabilities Planning Council demonstration project said they would take the projects on again and have made the commitment to continuing and expanding their parent resource centers based on the overwhelmingly positive community response.

There are four general sources of funding for establishing a parent resource center: government sources, private foundations, local groups and individuals, and library support.

Government sources. Federal, state, and local government agencies may be sources of funding for specific parent resource center services or for the program as a whole. Contacting agencies involved with the target audiences is recommended for learning about current funding opportunities. These include government agencies that oversee education and library services, developmental disabilities services, and youth, health, and social services. Many libraries have joined with other community groups to develop a broad response to community needs for which the library-based parent resource center is one aspect of a larger grant-funded project.

Private foundations. Private foundations are potential supporters of parent resource centers. It is important to identify those foundations interested in the populations or subjects that are to be targeted. Regional and local foundations, in particular, are interested in funding local organizations.

Information about foundation priorities and procedures can be obtained through the Foundation Center library. To find the closest site, write to the Foundation Center at 79 Fifth Avenue, New York, NY 10003, or call (800) 424–9836. When potential funders have been identified, write to them to get copies of their most recent guidelines for proposals.

For first-time grant writers, it may be good to think about recruiting a community volunteer to help. That is what several of the DDPC projects did. Maybe a library staff member could take a grantsmanship course or consultants from a regional library system may be able to help develop a proposal. Chapter 7 in *Serving Families and Children through Partnerships: A How-To-Do-It-Manual for Librarians* (Feinberg and Feldman, 1996) outlines specific steps in writing a proposal and discusses other ways of obtaining funding.

Local groups and individuals. Community groups were important contributors to parent resource center programs in all of the DDPC sites. In some cases, groups like the Kiwanis and Lions Clubs raised hundreds of dollars for the general support of a center. Others, such as Friends of the Library associations, designated their donations for space renovation or for the purchase of specific resource books or materials for workshop participants.

Community agencies, associations, and individuals found various ways to support the programs. Their contributions included parenting videos, materials on specific disabilities, and subscriptions to magazines. Individuals contributed their expertise to the program by leading seminars, speaking on panels, or being resources at workshops, as well as by assisting with collection development.

Ongoing library support. While outside funding may support the early phases of a project, maintaining a library-based parent resource center depends upon the people who make decisions about local library budgets and programs: town supervisors and boards, library trustees, and the library director.

Whether creating a specific budget line for the parent resource center or drawing on funds from existing lines to maintain services, it is important to establish internal procedures that assure that the needs of the parent resource center are incorporated into planning and resource allocation and acquisition. Parent resource center duties need to be incorporated into staff job descriptions to ensure that these tasks are continued.

GUIDELINES FOR DEVELOPING A PARENT COLLECTION

It is important to keep in mind that all parents need access to information and that parents of children with disabilities will benefit from the information found in a general parenting collection (e.g., child development, parenting skills, discipline techniques). For this reason, it is essential that information for parents of children with disabilities be integrated into general, inclusive collections for parents, enabling families with special needs to find these materials easily and, if desired, anonymously. Integrated collections enable parents to browse for resources without feeling embarrassed, uncomfortable, or different.

Special collections devoted to parenting concerns and family issues are very effective in promoting awareness of these resources and are particularly well located in a children's room where parents are regular and frequent visitors. Experience has shown some benefits to situating the collection adjacent to or within the children's section so that parents can keep an eye on youngsters while browsing for the information they need. Children's librarians come into direct contact with parents when they use the children's room and the familiarity can lessen the parent's intimidation at seeking assistance. Toys, available near parenting collection shelves, keep young children occupied while parents browse.

A detailed rationale and guidelines for developing comprehensive parent collections in public libraries can be found in Chapters 11 and 12 of *Serving Families and Children through Partnerships: A How-To-Do-It-Manual for Librarians* (Feinberg and Feldman, 1996).

TARGET AUDIENCE

The first step in building the collection is to determine the target audience. Will the resources be selected to meet the needs of parents only, or will the collection also be useful for professionals, such as child care workers who include children with disabilities in their homes and centers, classroom teachers, early intervention service providers, and preschool special education or health care workers (e.g., nurses, speech therapists, and physical therapists) providing services to children in homes, schools, and the community as well as in special facilities?

Even if it is determined that parents will be the primary focus of the collection, there will be decisions about the level of the material to be included. While a great deal of popularly written material is available for parents of children with disabilities, often the level of sophistication of the questions that parents bring to the library in their search for information requires access to reference material written primarily for professionals. Libraries must decide if they are able, or feel it is within their role, to provide access to this level of specialized material. As with all collections, consideration must be given to having materials that appeal to a multicultural/multilingual audience and meet the needs of those with limited literacy skills.

SCOPE

Collections for parents of children with disabilities and the professionals who work with them should include information on

- pregnancy and general child development;
- specific disabilities and health conditions;
- emotional, social, and financial issues of parents of children with disabilities;
- advocacy techniques and strategies;
- personal/biographical/experiential accounts written by parents;
- legal rights;
- hospitalization;
- coping with death and chronic illness;
- discipline, parenting skills, and behavior management;
- play and activities for children;
- needs of siblings;
- education issues;
- early intervention and family-centered care;
- communication between home and school, parent and professional;
- speech and language development;
- nutrition, feeding, safety, and health issues, especially as related to specific disabilities;
- family travel and recreation;
- sexuality education;
- child abuse prevention;
- toys, furniture, equipment, and technology;
- specific local services and organizations.

FORMATS

Regarding the types of materials to include, there are many issues to consider when building a collection.

1. In what formats will information be available?
2. Will print information include books, periodicals, and pamphlets, as well as brochures on local agencies and services?
3. If audiovisual material is available on general parenting information, will it be expanded to include videotape and audiocassette material specially produced for parents of children with disabilities?
4. Will access to specialized online databases and indexing services be available?
5. What about access to electronic resources via the Internet or a CD-ROM network that provide information and mutual support to parents and helping professionals?
6. Does the library use kits to package specific information for targeted audiences and, if so, will any special kits be developed and targeted to families of children with disabilities?
7. Is there a community information file in either print or computer format to assist parents and professionals to locate support groups and local services?

SELECTION CONSIDERATIONS

Will any form of needs assessment, user survey, or focus group be conducted to solicit input on either the subject or scope of the collection? Will parents or professionals working with families of children with disabilities be utilized to suggest or assess materials for the collection? User input is particularly helpful in selecting video material for purchase, given the considerable expense involved, and provides the added benefit of group viewing as a networking and community coalition-building activity. Information contained in this chapter about specific sources of print and audiovisual material about children with disabilities and their families should prove helpful in locating reliable information from which to choose.

Keep in mind that currency is critical with health- and disability-related information as well as the reliability of the reference source. Using reputable publishers, authoritative sources such as national organizations devoted to a specific disability, or authors who are specialists affiliated with well-known research facilities assures the reliability of the information. The level of the material, whether highly technical or written for the layperson, is another consideration although perhaps less important if the information is very rare and difficult to find.

REFERENCE MATERIALS FOR PARENTS AND PROFESSIONALS

Many of the specialized resources containing health and medical information sought after by parents and professionals are most suitable as "Reference Only," whether in a specially designated section of the Parents Collection or within the library's general Reference Collection. Their content, organization, and costliness usually make them unsuitable for circulation. The following sections include topics and possible reference selections that anticipate many of the reference questions presented by parents of children with disabilities.

GENERAL READY REFERENCE FOR PARENTS

Sources such as Franck and Brownstone's *Parenting A to Z* (New York: HarperCollins, 1996), previously published as the *Parents' Desk Reference*; Starer's *Who to Call: The Parent's Source Book* (New York: William Morrow, 1992) and Beth DeFrancis's *The Parents' Resource Almanac* (Holbrook, Mass.: Adams Publishing, 1994) are compendiums of information that can provide quick access to the name and address of an organization, a definition, and so forth. Although not devoted specifically to disability issues and information, these books serve well as a first resource and can often make further search unnecessary; they are particularly good choices for small libraries with limited budgets where there is little possibility of purchasing specialized resources for parents.

MEDICAL ENCYCLOPEDIAS AND DICTIONARIES

There are many medical reference tools, including the *Marshall Cavendish Encyclopedia of Family Health* (New York: Marshall Cavendish, 1993); *Mayo Clinic Family Health Book* (New York: William Morrow, 1996); *Physicians' Guide to Rare Diseases* (Montvale, N.J.: Dowden, 1995); *Dictionary of Developmental Disabilities Terminology* (Baltimore: Paul H. Brookes, 1996); *American Medical Association Family Medical Guide* (New York: Random House, 1994).

REFERENCES ON CHILDHOOD DISABILITIES, ILLNESSES, AND SYNDROMES

In addition to reference sources, other materials include *Children with Disabilities: A Medical Primer*, 4th edition (Baltimore: Paul H. Brookes, 1997); *Smith's Recognizable Pattern of Human Malformation* (Philadelphia: W.B. Saunders, 1996); Gilbert's *A-Z Reference Book of Syndromes and Inherited Disorders* (San Diego: Singular Publishing, 1995); *Encyclopedia of Genetic Disorders and Birth Defects* (New

York: Facts on File, 1991); *Diseases of the Nervous System in Childhood* (New York: Cambridge University Press, 1992); *Infectious Diseases of Children* (Baltimore: Mosby Year Book, 1992); *Schaffer and Avery's Diseases of the Newborn* (Philadelphia: W.B. Saunders, 1991); Blackman's *Medical Aspects of Developmental Disabilities in Children Birth to Three*, 3rd edition (Gaithersburg, Md.: Aspen Publishers, 1997); *Jolly's Diseases of Children* (Malden, Mass.: Blackwell Science, 1991); Buyse's *Birth Defects Encyclopedia* (Malden, Mass.: Blackwell Science, 1992); *The Classification of Child and Adolescent Mental Diagnosis in Primary Care: Diagnostic and Statistical Manual for Primary Care (DSM-PC): Child and Adolescent Version* (Elk Grove Village, Ill.: American Academy of Pediatrics, 1996) and *Diagnostic and Statistical Manual of Mental Disorders: DSM I* (Washington D.C.: American Psychiatric Association, 1994); *Diagnostic Classification of Mental Health and Developmental Disorders of Infancy and Early Childhood* (Washington D.C.: Zero to Three National Center for Infants, Toddlers and Families, 1994); Cohen and Volkmar's *Handbook of Autism and Pervasive Developmental Disorders* (New York: John Wiley and Sons, 1997).

GUIDES TO SCHOOLS, FACILITIES, ORGANIZATIONS, AND EQUIPMENT FOR CHILDREN WITH SPECIAL NEEDS

An excellent resource guide to products, national organizations, and services for children with disabilities, published on an annual basis, is *Exceptional Parent* (Brookline, Mass.: Psy-Ed Corporation). A series of guides is published by Grey House Publishing (Lakeville, Conn.) including *Complete Directory for People with Disabilities* (1996), *Complete Directory for People with Chronic Illness* (1994), and *Complete Learning Disabilities Directory: Products, Resources, Books, Services* (1996). Other sources include the *Directory for Exceptional Children: A Listing of Educational and Training Facilities* (Boston: Porter-Sargent, 1994); the *BOSC Directory: Facilities for People with Learning Disabilities* (Congers, N.Y.: BOSC Publishers, 1996); the *AAUP Resource Guide to Organizations Concerned with Developmental Handicaps* (Silver Spring, Md.: American Association of University Affiliated Programs for Persons with Developmental Disabilities, 1994); the *Self-Help Sourcebook: Finding and Forming Mutual Aid Self-Help Groups* (Denville, N.J.: American Self-Help Clearinghouse, 1995); and *Help for Children: From Infancy to Adulthood: A National Directory of Hotlines, Organizations, Agencies, and Other Resources* (Shepherdstown, W.Va.: Rocky River Publishers, 1995). Having catalogs of distributors of special equipment, toys, and assistive devices available for parents to borrow or use in the library can also be very helpful.

CHILDREN'S LITERATURE GUIDES

In addition to the bibliography of children's books related to the theme of inclusion found in Appendix A, some excellent listings of books for children on disability issues appear in *Kids with Special Needs: Information and Activities to Promote Awareness and Understanding* (Santa Barbara, Calif.: The Learning Works, 1996). The classic sources for locating books for children and teens on disability issues remain *Portraying Persons with Disabilities: An Annotated Bibliography of Nonfiction for Children and Teenagers* by Joan Brest Friedberg et al. (New Providence, N.J.: R.R. Bowker, 1992) and *Portraying Persons with Disabilities: An Annotated Bibliography of Fiction for Children and Teenagers* by Debra Robertson (New Providence, N.J.: R.R. Bowker, 1992). Useful as well is *Sensitive Issues: An Annotated Guide to Children's Literature K-6* by Timothy Rasinski and Cindy Gillespie (Phoenix: Oryx Press, 1992), which devotes a section to dealing with illness and disability. Whether utilized by the parent or the librarian, *A to Zoo: Subject Access to Children's Picture Books* (New Providence, N.J.: R.R. Bowker, 1993); *The Bookfinder: A Guide to Children's Literature about the Needs and Problems of Youth Aged 2–15* (Circle Pines, Minn.: American Guidance Service, 1994); and Rudman et al.'s *Books to Help Children Cope with Separation and Loss* (New Providence, N.J.: R.R. Bowker, 1994) can help parents find books to help children cope with both typical and exceptional childhood situations and stresses.

TESTING RESOURCES

David Wodrich's *Children's Psychological Testing: A Guide for Nonpsychologists* (Baltimore: Paul H. Brookes, 1997); McCollough's *Testing and Your Child: What You Should Know about 150 of the Most Common Medical, Educational and Psychological Tests* (New York: Plume, 1992); and *Tests: A Comprehensive Reference for Assessments in Psychology, Education and Business*, edited by Sweetland and Keyser (Austin, Tex.: Pro-Ed, 1997), contain information on sources for testing.

CHILDREN'S MEDICATIONS

Information on medication for children is provided in *PDR Family Guide to Prescription Drugs* (New York: Crown Publishing Group, 1996); Griffith and Elsberry's *Complete Guide to Prescription and Nonprescription Pediatric Drugs: A Parent's Concise Reference to Drugs for Infants through Adolescents* (New York: Berkeley Publications, 1996); Bates and Nahata's *Children's Medications: A Parent's Guide* (Cincinnati, Ohio: Harvey Whitney Books, 1995).

LEGAL ISSUES FOR PARENTS

Early Intervention Regulation: Annotation and Analysis (Horsham, Pa.: LRP Publications, 1994); Tucker and Goldstein's *Educational Rights of Children with Disabilities: Analysis, Decisions and Commentary* (Horsham, Pa.: LRP Publications, 1993); Ordover and Boundy's *Educational Rights of Children with Disabilities: A Primer for Advocates* (Boston, Mass.: Center for Law and Education, 1991); and Turnbull's *Free Appropriate Public Education* (Denver, Colo.: Love Publishing Co., 1993) provide parents with legal information.

GUIDES TO CAMPS, RECREATION FACILITIES, AND FAMILY ACTIVITIES

Resources for Children with Special Needs, Inc. in New York City puts out an annual *Special Camp Guide: Camps and Summer Programs for Children with Special Needs* in both English and Spanish. Though weighted heavily toward the New York City/New York State area, the guide does include many out-of-state camps as well as a good listing of camp guides put out by other organizations, including the Learning Disabilities Association of America, Candlelighters Childhood Cancer Foundation, National Hemophilia Foundation, American Diabetes Foundation, National Easter Seal Society, and the American Foundation for the Blind. Any guides to local recreational programs, camps, and activities are especially useful and make welcome additions to the parents collection.

GOVERNMENT PUBLICATIONS

Government publications, particularly those available from sources like state education, social service, and health departments, provide information on statewide early intervention and special education regulations, local health regulations, and entitlement program benefit information (Medicaid, SSI, etc.). This information is valuable to parents and often difficult for the average citizen to locate. These state-level agencies usually have publication departments that provide lists of available documents, reports, and so forth that can be ordered free of charge.

ORDERING SOURCES FOR PARENT AND PROFESSIONAL MATERIALS

Standard reviewing sources that are traditionally utilized for general library ordering (e.g., *Booklist*, *Library Journal*, and *Publishers Weekly*), feature reviews of popular trade books that are of interest to parents, including materials of special interest to parents of children with disabilities. Look for them primarily under the "Psychology," "Education," "Home Economics," and "Health and Medicine" adult nonfiction reviews. The newest titles by well-known authors and the largest publishing houses will be reviewed in these standard reviewing sources.

If the library subscribes to magazines and newsletters aimed especially at parents of children with disabilities, for example, *Exceptional Parent*, these are excellent sources of new materials in book, audiovisual, and pamphlet format. Many of these special publications feature review sections, bibliographies, or book lists attached to feature articles. Because these publications appeal to a very targeted audience, they are among the best sources of the latest and most highly recommended titles in specific disability- and health-related subject areas. If at all possible, have someone on staff assigned to review specific periodicals on a regular basis, noting new and recommended items for purchase. A listing of newsletters and periodicals specifically directed at parents and professionals around health and disability issues appears later in this chapter.

An excellent and comprehensive "Special Needs Collection" for parents of children with disabilities and chronic health conditions is put out by Woodbine House. This source, along with the Barnes and Noble collection, the *Exceptional Parent Library* and the *Books on Special Children* are excellent sources of materials for parents. Paul H. Brookes, Brunner-Mazel, Charles C. Thomas, and Guilford Publications are excellent sources of professionally oriented materials that may have great appeal to parents. Addresses for all of these publishers are cited in the bibliographies. Many organizations and small presses specialize in information on specific health, disability, or related topics of interest to parents and professionals. If room can be found, it's a good idea to request catalogs from these sources, review them for additions to the collection, and file them alphabetically in a file drawer. They can be invaluable to have on hand when searching for materials on a specific subject. You may even want to consider having the catalogs themselves available for parents to review or even borrow as they may be interested in these special sources for personal ordering.

DISABILITY AND HEALTH ISSUES

Alexander Graham Bell Association for the Deaf, 3417 Volta Place NW, Washington DC 20007–2778; (202) 337–5220

American Academy of Pediatrics, PO Box 927, Elk Grove Village, IL 60009–0927; (800) 433–9016

American Diabetes Association, 1660 Duke Street, Alexandria, VA 22314; (800) 232–3472

American Foundation for the Blind, 11 Penn Plaza, Suite 300, New York, NY 10001; (212) 502–7600

American Printing House for the Blind, PO Box 6085, 1879 Frankfurt Avenue, Louisville, KY 40206–0085; (800) 223–1839

Association for the Care of Children's Health (ACCH), 7910 Woodmont Avenue, Bethesda, MD 20814–3015; (301) 654–6549 or (800) 808–ACCH

Autism Society of America, 7910 Woodmont Avenue, Suite 650, Bethesda, MD 20814; (800) 328–8476

Autism Society of North Carolina, 505 Oberlin Road, Suite 230, Raleigh, NC 27605–1345; (800) 442–2762 or (919) 743–0204

Barnes and Noble Special Needs Collection, 122 Fifth Avenue, New York, NY 10010; (212) 633–4093

Beach Center on Families and Disability, University of Kansas, 3111 Haworth, Lawrence, KS 66045; (913) 864–7600

Blind Children's Center, 4120 Marathon Street, Los Angeles, CA 90029; (800) 222–3566 or (213) 664–2153

Books on Special Children (BOSC), PO Box 305, Congers, NY 10920–0305; (914) 638–1236

Brookes Publishing Company (formerly Paul H. Brookes), PO Box 10624, Baltimore, MD 21285; (800) 638–3775

Brookline Books, PO Box 1046, Cambridge, MA 02238; (617) 868–0360

Candlelighters Childhood Cancer Foundation, 7910 Woodmont Drive, Suite 460, Bethesda, MD 20814–3015; (301) 657–8401

Charles C. Thomas Publisher, PO Box 19265, 2600 South First Street, Springfield, IL 62794–9265; (800) 258–8980

Council for Exceptional Children, 1920 Association Drive, Reston, VA 20191–1589; (703) 620–3660

Epilepsy Foundation of America, 4351 Garden City Drive, Landover, MD 20785; (301) 459–3700

Exceptional Parent Library, Dept. EPCAT4, PO Box 8045, Brick, NJ 08723; (800) 535–1910

Federation for Children with Special Needs, 95 Berkeley Street, Suite 104, Boston, MA 02116; (800) 331–0688

HEATH National Clearinghouse on Postsecondary Education for Individuals with Disabilities, c/o HEATH/American Council on

Education, Dept. 36, Washington DC 20055–0036; (202) 939–9320; gopher://bobcat-ace.nche.edu; http://www.acenet.edu

Let's Face It Resource List, Box 29972, Bellingham, WA 98228–1972; (360) 676–7325

March of Dimes Birth Defects Foundation, 1275 Mamaroneck Avenue, White Plains, NY 10605; (914) 428–7100

National Association for Parents of the Visually Impaired, PO Box 317, Watertown, MA 02272; (800) 562–6265

National Association of the Deaf, 814 Thayer Avenue, Silver Springs, MD 20910; (301) 587–1788

National Down Syndrome Society, 666 Broadway, New York, NY 10012; (800) 221–4602

National Easter Seal Society, 230 West Monroe, Suite 1800, Chicago, IL 60606; (312) 726–6200

National Hemophilia Foundation, 110 Greene Street, Suite 406, New York, NY 10012; (212) 219–8180 or (800) 424–2634

National Information Center for Children and Youth With Disabilities (NICHCY), PO Box 1492, Washington DC 20013–1492; (800) 695–0285; http://www.nichcy.org

National Lekotek Center, 2100 Ridge Avenue, Evanston, IL 60204; (708) 328–0001

National Maternal and Child Health Clearinghouse, 2070 Chain Bridge Road, Suite 450, Vienna, VA 22182; (703) 356–1964; e-mail NMCHC@circsol.com

National Organization for Rare Disorders (NORD), PO Box 8923, New Fairfield, CT 06812–8923; (203) 746–6518

National Parent Network on Disabilities, 1727 King Street, Suite 305, Alexandria, VA 22314; (703) 684–6763

Pacer Center, Inc., 4826 Chicago Avenue S., Minneapolis, MN 55417–1098; (612) 827–2966; http://www.pacer.org

Pediatric Projects, PO Box 571555, Tarzana, CA 91357–1555; (800) 947–0947

Pro-Ed, 8700 Shoal Creek Boulevard, Austin, TX 78757–6897; (512) 451–3246

TASH: The Association for Persons with Severe Handicaps, 29 West Susquehanna Avenue, Suite 210, Baltimore, MD 21204; (410) 828–8274

Therapy Skill Builders, c/o Psychological Corporation, 555 Academic Court, San Antonio, TX 78204; (800) 211–8378

Tourette Syndrome Association, Inc., 42–40 Bell Boulevard, Suite 205, Bayside, NY 11361–2820; (718) 224–2999

United Cerebral Palsy Association, 1660 L Street NW, Suite 700, Washington DC 20036–5602; (202) 776–0406

Visually Impaired Preschool Services, 1229 Garvin Place, Louisville, KY 40203; (502) 636–3207

VORT Corporation, PO Box 60132, Palo Alto, CA 94306; (415) 322–8282; http://www.vort.com

Woodbine House, 6510 Bells Mill Road, Bethesda, MD 20817; (800) 843–7323

Young Adult Institute (YAI), 460 West 34th Street, New York, NY 10001; (212) 563–7474

DEATH AND BEREAVEMENT

Centering Corporation, 1531 North Saddle Creek Road, Omaha, NE 68104–5064; (402) 553–1200

Compassionate Friends, PO Box 3696, Oak Brook, IL 60522–3696; (630) 990–0010

LANGUAGE AND SPEECH

American Speech-Language-Hearing Association, 10801 Rockville Pike, Rockville, MD 20852; (301) 897–5700

Center for Speech and Language Disorders, 479 Spring Road, Elmhurst, IL 60126; (708) 530–8551

Communication Skill Builders, c/o Psychological Corporation, 555 Academic Street, San Antonio, TX 78204; (800) 211–8378

LEARNING DISABILITIES

A.D.D. Warehouse, 300 Northwest 70th Avenue, Suite 102, Plantation, FL 33317; (954) 792–8944

Children and Adults with Attention Deficit Disorders (CHADD), 499 NW 70th Avenue, Suite 308, Plantation, FL 33317; (305) 587–3700

Learning Disabilities Association of America, 4156 Library Road, Pittsburgh, PA 15234; (412) 341–1515

National Center for Learning Disabilities, 381 Park Avenue South, Suite 142, New York, NY 10016; (212) 545–7510

MENTAL HEALTH

American Academy of Child and Adolescent Psychiatry, 3615 Wisconsin Avenue NW, Washington, DC 20016; (202) 966–7300

Brunner-Mazel, 19 Union Square West, New York, NY 10003; (212) 924–3344

Guilford Publications, 72 Spring Street, New York, NY 10012; (212) 431–9800

PERIODICALS

Specialized newsletters and periodicals written specially for parents of children with specific disabilities and health conditions abound and can be excellent sources of the most up-to-date theories and research, new technologies, treatments, legal and entitlement information, and so forth. They often include parent-to-parent and new publications sections, and are important additions to any collections aimed at parents of children with special needs. If restricted to one title, the standout is *Exceptional Parent*, noted for its overall quality and the breadth of its coverage (as it is not restricted to any one disability area). The following list includes magazines, newsletters, and journals that may be of particular interest to parents of children with disabilities or professionals working with them. An asterisk (*) denotes those of particular interest to professionals or those with a more academic, research, or practitioner orientation.

ACCH Advocate, Association for the Care of Children's Health, 7910 Woodmont Avenue, Bethesda, MD 20814; (301) 654–6549.

ADHD Report, Guilford Press, 72 Spring Street, New York, NY 10012; (800) 365–7006

Attention!, C.H.A.D.D. (Children and Adults with Attention Deficit Disorders), 499 NW 70th Avenue, Plantation, FL 33317; (305) 587–3700

Brown University Child and Adolescent Behavior Letter, 208 Governor Street, Providence, RI 02906; (800) 333–7771

Candlelighters Quarterly Newsletter, Childhood Cancer Foundation, c/o American Cancer Society, 7910 Woodmont Avenue, Suite 460, Bethesda, MD 20814–3015; (301) 657–8401; (800) 366–2223

Child Care Plus+, Montana University Affiliated Rural Institute on Disabilities, 52 Corbin Hall, University of Montana, Missoula MT 59812; (800) 235–4122

***Children's Health Care**, Journal of the Association for the Care of Children's Health, c/o Lawrence Erlbaum Associates, 10 Industrial Avenue, Mahwah, NJ 07430–2262; call ACCH (301) 654–6549

Countdown, Juvenile Diabetes Foundation International, 120 Wall Street, New York, NY 10005–4001; (800) 223–1138; (212) 785–9500

Down Syndrome News, National Down Syndrome Congress, 1605 Chantilly Drive, Suite 250, Atlanta, GA 30324

Early Childhood Report: Children with Special Needs and Their Families, LRP Publications, 747 Dresher Road, PO Box 980, Horsham, PA 19044–0980; (800) 341–7874, ext. 275

Early Intervention, Illinois Early Childhood Intervention Clearinghouse, 830 South Spring Street, Springfield, IL 62704; (217) 785–1364

The Endeavor, American Society for Deaf Children, 2848 Arden Way, Suite 210, Sacramento, CA 95825–1373; (800) 942–ASDC

*Exceptional Children, The Council for Exceptional Children, 1920 Association Drive, Reston, VA 20191–1589; (800) 232–7323

Exceptional Parent, PO Box 3000, Denville, NJ 07834–9919; (800) 562–1973

Families and Disability Newsletter, University of Kansas, Beach Center on Families and Disability, 3111 Haworth Hall, Lawrence, KS 66045–7516; (913) 864–7600

Future Reflections, National Federation of the Blind Magazine for Parents of Blind Children, 1800 Johnson Street, Baltimore, MD 21230; (410) 659–9314

*Inclusive Education Programs: Advice on Educating Students with Disabilities in Regular Settings, LRP Publications, 747 Dresher Road, Suite 500, Horsham, PA 19044–0980; (215) 784–0941

*Infants & Young Children: Interdisciplinary Journal of Special Care Practices, Aspen Publishers, 7201 McKinney Circle, Frederick, MD 21704; (800) 638–8437

LDA Newsbriefs, Learning Disabilities Association, 4156 Library Road, Pittsburgh, PA 15234; (412) 341–1515

M A Report, Allergy and Asthmatics Network, Mothers of Asthmatics, Inc., 3554 Chain Bridge Road, Suite 200, Fairfax, VA 22030–2709; (800) 878–4403

Mainstream: Magazine of the Able-Disabled, PO Box 370598, San Diego, CA 92137–0598

NICHCY News Digest, National Information Center for Children and Youth with Disabilities, PO Box 1492, Washington DC 20013–1492; (800) 695–0285

Pacesetter, PACER Center, 4826 Chicago Avenue S., Minneapolis, MN 55417–1098; (800) 537–2237

Pediatric Mental Health, Pediatric Projects, PO Box 571555, Tarzana, CA 91357; (800) 947–0947

*Pediatrics, official publication of the American Academy of Pediatrics, PO Box 927, Elk Grove Village, IL 60009–0927; (847) 228–5005

Pediatrics for Parents, PO Box 1069, Bangor, ME 04402–1069; (207) 942–6212

The Roundtable, Journal of the National Resource Center for Special Needs Adoption, 16250 Northland Drive, Suite 120, Southfield, MI 48075; (810) 443–7080

Sibling Information Network Newsletter, University of Connecticut, A.J. Pappanikou Center, 249 Glenbrook Road, U-64, Storrs, CT 06269–2064; (860) 486–0273

Superkids: A Newsletter for Families and Friends of Children with Limb Differences, 60 Clyde Street, Newton, MA 02160

*__Washington Watch,__ United Cerebral Palsy Associations, 1660 L Street NW, Suite 700, Washington DC 20036; (800) USA-5UCP

Wide Smiles (for information and networking among families of cleft children), PO Box 5153, Stockton, CA 95205–0153; (209) 942–2812

AUDIOVISUALS

The increasing affordability and popularity of video materials for parents, and their potential for reaching the nonreading parent, make videos an important consideration for the parents collection. Agency professionals often look for videos for group programming because parent instruction in specific care techniques can be very effective in video format.

The quality of videotape material varies widely and can best be evaluated by previewing. In addition, reliance on reviews and endorsement from reliable organizations and authorities in the field helps to ensure quality and accuracy. Using parents and local specialists who work with families of children with disabilities to preview video material and make recommendations can be a good way of soliciting informed feedback, creating awareness of the availability of these materials to potential users and reinforcing partnerships with local community agencies. In general, the basic criteria for evaluating video material are

- accuracy and currency of information;
- technical quality/appeal of the presentation;
- suitability for intended audience;
- cultural/social limitations of the presentation;
- length/ability to hold viewer's attention;
- cost/affordability.

Both *Booklist* and *Library Journal* review audiovisual material, often including titles appropriate for family support collections specifically of interest to parents of children with disabilities. Many of the specific disability-focused organizations listed in the ordering sources earlier in this chapter include video material in their resource catalogs. Jordan and Stackpole's *Audiovisual Resources for Family Programming* (New York: Neal-Schuman, 1994) includes annotations on hundreds of video titles specifically for parents of children with disabilities and chronic health conditions.

There are many distributors of video material that specialize in disability and health issues suitable for parent/professional collections. Don't hesitate to speak to the company's sales representative if the price is beyond reach. They sometimes have latitude to strike a "deal," especially for regular customers or when ordered in quantity. Here are some good sources that specialize in or regularly include video material suitable for parents of children with disabilities:

Association for the Care of Children's Health (ACCH), 7910 Woodmont Avenue, Suite 300, Bethesda, MD 20814; (800) 808–2224

Child Development Media, 5632 Van Nuys Boulevard, Suite 286, Van Nuys, CA 91401; (800) 405–8942

Comforty Media Concepts, 2145 Pioneer Road, Evanston, IL 60201; (847) 475–0791

Educational Productions, 7412 SW Beaverton Hillsdale Highway, Suite 210, Portland, OR 97225; (800) 950–4949

Fanlight Productions, 47 Halifax Street, Boston, MA 02130; (617) 524–0980

Films for the Humanities & Sciences, PO Box 2053, Princeton, NJ 08543–2053; (609) 275–1400

Guilford Publications, 72 Spring Street, New York, NY 10012; (212) 431–9800

James Stanfield Publishing Company, Drawer 124, PO Box 41058, Santa Barbara, CA 93140; (800) 421–6534

Learner Managed Designs, PO Box 747, Lawrence, KS 66044; (913) 842–9088

Polymorph, 95 Chapel Street, Newton, MA 02158; (800) 370–3456

Universal Health Communications, 1200 S. Federal Highway, Suite 202, Boynton Beach, FL 33435; (561) 731–5881 or (800) 229–1842

Vida Health Communications, 6 Bigelow Street, Cambridge, MA 02139; (617) 864–4334

Young Adult Institute (YAI), 460 West 34th Street, New York, NY 10001; (212) 563–7474

VERTICAL FILE

A vertical file offers the best way to organize ephemeral materials like pamphlets, articles, and reports for easy access by parents and professionals. Arranged by subject in a file drawer, and devoted to topics of interest to parents, this is a relatively inexpensive way of keeping information on hand, particularly if financial resources prohibit large book or media collections focused on parenting topics. Vertical files are especially useful for information that is so new and current that little or nothing is available yet in book format, or for very specific and difficult-to-locate subjects. Parents of children with disabilities are often looking for just this type of information. Long before there were books on fragile X syndrome, elective mutism, oppositional defiant disorder, the Americans with Disabilities Act, or facilitated communication, articles and pamphlets were available. Because the vertical file should reflect current, new information, it needs to be weeded regularly. Since it has no real visual appeal, it will usually go overlooked unless the librarian draws the parents' attention to it.

Readily available access to the Internet or to full-text electronic access to a large selection of periodicals may reduce the need to maintain a vertical file. Chapter 12 describes Internet sites of special interest to parents of children with disabilities. If a vertical file is to be developed, begin by using a preprinted postcard or form letter, sending requests for free single copies of resources to some of the national organizations listed in the ordering sources above. Many national organizations provide extensive amounts of information free of charge for the asking. NICHCY (the National Information Center for Children and Youth with Disabilities) (PO Box 1492, Washington DC 20013–1492; (800) 695–0285; http://www.nichcy.org) is a good place to start. The "ready reference" tools listed in the reference section above include hundreds of organizations that provide appropriate and free material suitable for a parents' vertical file.

Don't overlook including brochures describing local area agencies, services, support groups, early intervention programs, community recreation facilities, and so forth, that may be of particular interest to parents, especially parents of children with disabilities. Most agencies welcome the exposure and will send quantities for your display rack as well as your vertical file, free of charge. This is a wonderfully inexpensive way of making the library the connecting point between the family and all of those community resources that parents may very much need but of which they may be totally unaware. It also reminds the health and human service providers that libraries are the information centers for families. Consequently, they may begin to envision other ways of connecting with you on behalf of families.

KITS

There are various ways of packaging, presenting, and guiding people to information in the family support collection in order to increase access, awareness, and utilization of materials. Kits provide an opportunity to assemble a variety of materials on a specific theme or with a specific focus and package them together so they're attractive and easy to use. Particular audiences can be targeted and the time-consuming task of material selection, often when the patron is in a rush, with children in tow, can be avoided. Kits can be developed to welcome new babies, provide pregnant moms with prenatal and early infant care information, help parents occupy sick-at-home kids, provide curriculum support for family day care providers, or assist grandparents with visiting grandchildren. The possibilities are endless.

Libraries can design kits to circulate, packaged in plastic or cardboard containers, or plastic, cloth, or mesh bags. Kits can also be intended as giveaways, to be kept by the patron, packaged in large paper envelopes and printed with colorful logos, illustrations, and decorative borders for eye-catching appeal. Kits of either type can be developed to especially meet the needs of parents of children with disabilities. A few examples include a hospital kit or an early intervention family resource kit.

HOSPITAL KIT

A circulating hospital kit, targeted to parents of children entering the hospital, may contain

- Picture books with a "going to the hospital" theme for parents to read aloud to young children.
- Pamphlets designed for parents to help their child prepare for and cope with this experience, available from ACCH, 7910 Woodmont Avenue, Suite 300, Bethesda, MD 20814; (800) 808–2224.
- Bibliography of books available in the library on preparing children for the hospital experience.
- Videos for children on the hospital experience including (Mister Rogers' *Going to the Hospital*, available from Family Communications, 4802 Fifth Avenue, Pittsburgh, PA 15213; (412) 687–2990).
- Hands-on activities to do in the hospital, e.g., "Fuzzy Felt Hospital" or "The Hospital Game," available from Pediatric Projects, PO Box 571555, Tarzana, CA 91357–1555; (800) 947–0947.

EARLY INTERVENTION FAMILY RESOURCE KIT

An early intervention family resource kit can be provided as a give-away to parents who are concerned that their young child might have some type of developmental delay or are aware that their young child has a disability. The kit might include

- Brochures and flyers on local early intervention services, the early intervention process, and the family's rights within the system.
- A developmental milestones checklist that provides information on the stages of development and typical ages for arriving at certain milestones is available in Appendix B; order "Developmental Checklist for Young Children: Birth to Five Years" from The ARC, 500 E. Border Street, Suite 300, Arlington, TX 76010, or "Are You Listening to What Your Child May Not Be Saying" from the National Easter Seal Society, 230 West Monroe, Suite 1800, Chicago, IL 60606; (312) 726–6200.
- The NICHCY (National Information Center for Children and Youth with Disabilities), publications list of free materials for parents, as well as the appropriate state resource sheet; a separate resource list is available for every state. Contact: NICHCY, PO Box 1492, Washington DC 20013–1492; (800) 695–0285; http://www.aed.org/nichcy.
- Issue of *NICHCY News Digest* (Vol. III, No.1, 1993), "You Are Not Alone: For Parents When They Learn that Their Child Has a Disability" and "Parenting a Child with Special Needs: A Guide to Readings and Resources."
- Information on local parent support groups, a local parent-to-parent network, advocacy training opportunities, the local family consumer council, etc.
- Bibliographies of library materials of special interest for parents of children with disabilities.
- A listing of the parenting and early childhood programs available at the library.

As the family support collection grows and develops, consider adding additional "access enhancers" to draw attention to those family resources that are specially of interest to parents of children with disabilities. Through bibliographies, booklists, brochures, and fliers, specific library resources can be highlighted to maximize awareness and use. Provide the school district and local agencies with copies of the library's brochures. Contact them by phone or in person. Don't assume that even "regulars" are aware of all there is to offer. Marketing needs to be ongoing and diverse.

RESOURCES

Feinberg, Sandra and Sari Feldman. 1996. *Serving Families and Children through Partnerships: A How-To-Do-It Manual*. New York: Neal-Schuman.

Jordan, Barbara and Noreen Stackpole. 1994. *Audiovisual Resources for Family Programming*. New York: Neal-Schuman.

Klauber, Julie and Avery Klauber. 1996. *Inclusion & Parent Advocacy: A Resource Guide*. Centereach, N.Y.: Disability Resources, with support from the New York State Developmental Disabilities Planning Council.

Steele, Barbara and Carolyn Willard. 1989. *Guidelines for Establishing a Family Resource Library*. Washington, D.C.: Association for the Care of Children's Health.

Walling, Linda Lucas and Marilyn H. Karrenbrock. 1993. *Disabilities, Children, and Libraries: Mainstreaming Services in Public Libraries and School Library Media Centers*. Englewood, CO: Libraries Unlimited.

Note: There is an extensive bibliography of books, articles, and audiovisual materials on inclusion for parents, children, librarians, and other professionals, located in the appendix, that will be of special interest to those establishing collections for parents and professionals.

REFERENCES

Cohen, Bonnie P. and Linda S. Simkin. 1994. *Library-Based Parent Resource Centers: A Guide To Implementing Programs*. Albany, N.Y.: New York State Developmental Disabilities Planning Council and the New York Library Association.

Feinberg, Sandra and Kathleen Deerr. 1994. *Running a Parent/Child Workshop: A How-To-Do-It Manual for Librarians*. New York: Neal-Schuman.

Jordan, Barbara. 1996. "Building a Family Support Collection: Guidelines" and "Building a Family Support Collection: Print and Nonprint Resources." In S. Feinberg and S. Feldman's *Serving Families and Children through Partnerships: A How-To-Do-It Manual for Librarians*. New York: Neal-Schuman: 117–158.

Lobosco, Anna F., Susan Keitel, Bonnie Primus Cohen, and Linda Simkin. "Serving Families in the Community: Library-Based Parent Resource Centers." *Public Libraries* (September/October 1996): 298–305.

Steele, Barbara and Carolyn Willard. 1989. *Guidelines for Establishing a Family Resource Library*. Washington, D.C.: Association for the Care of Children's Health.

12 ELECTRONIC RESOURCES

The Internet has opened up a whole world of support and information for those who are disabled, their families, and the helping professionals involved in their lives. One of the most important functions that the Internet offers is e-mail, the ability to transmit messages across the globe in a matter of minutes at a fraction of the cost of telephoning. Most Web sites, and especially disability-related sites, offer viewers the opportunity to "chat" or send e-mail to others viewing the site or to the developers of the site. This ability to reach out and communicate with others confronting some of the same challenges is particularly helpful in overcoming the feelings of isolation so often expressed by parents of children with disabilities. The Internet service provider that libraries or patrons choose usually offers e-mail as a basic service included in the monthly fee. By having an e-mail address, individuals are able to send and receive messages from those participating in bulletin boards, discussion groups, and other forums.

The second important function offered by the Internet is the access to worldwide information and resources. The wealth of information, full-text databases, and links helps librarians and families of children with disabilities to locate information on even the rarest of topics.

This chapter will give a brief overview of the Internet to help those who are just learning the ropes, including a few basic caveats regarding Internet addresses. These guidelines will also serve as a refresher to those who are "old hands" at this new technology. The bulk of the chapter provides information on a sampling of comprehensive, disability-related sites that are available on the World Wide Web.

NAVIGATING THE INTERNET

In a nutshell, every Internet Web page has an address called a Uniform Resource Locator (URL). This address contains information that the computer needs to identify and locate sites: server software, the domain name, and the directory path where the information is stored. Understanding the information contained in the URL will aid librarians in explaining this new language to patrons.

Every URL begins with a codename for the type of server software used to access a particular Web site. The four most common types are

- **Gophers:** The oldest method of manipulating files on the Internet (provides text-only access to a list of files stored in a server).
- **http (Hypertext Transfer Protocol):** The server software used by the World Wide Web.

- **FTP (File Transfer Protocol):** The Internet foundation, which other software use to move files.
- **News-server software:** Allows viewers to access news groups.

The domain name is the name chosen by the developer of each Web site. Each domain name must be registered with InterNIC, the central Internet authority. In registering a domain name, each site is given an extension that describes to whom or to what type of enterprise or institution the site belongs. Some extensions users should be familiar with include:

.com	site belonging to a commercial enterprise
.org	nonprofit entity
.edu	educational organization or institution
.lib	library
.gov	site belonging to either a local, state, or federal governmental agency
.mil	site belonging to a military institution
.net	site belonging to a network
.us	extension that describes a particular country (as, in this case, U.S. for the United States).

The URL gives the exact directory path (indicating in which directory of each domain name the files that the viewer is requesting are located). Often sites have multiple access points or particular files that store specific information. Some files are managed by individuals whose names may be posted as part of the URL address. In any case, two points need to be kept in mind when searching the Internet:

1. **It is critical that patrons type URLs exactly as they appear.** Addresses often contain blended words, a mixture of upper and lower cases, acronyms, and other identifiers such as hyphens and accent marks. Internet browsers are extremely sensitive to case and spacing. A *single* error in typing the address makes the site inaccessible.
2. **Internet addresses change on a rather frequent basis.** The reasons for the change vary, but might include the following:
   - those owning the Web page might have changed to another Internet service provider.
   - Another directory had to be created to accommodate a growing site.
   - The people who created the Web page have moved to another agency but are taking the Web site with them.

Most Web sites will post a message when they have moved or

changed their address. Usually, they will also provide a link to the new address; however, sometimes those links fail and users will have to type out a new URL in order to access the site. As a result, it is important to keep abreast of Web address changes.

DISABILITY-RELATED ELECTRONIC RESOURCES

There are hundreds of disability-related sites on the Internet. This listing of 50 sites is just a sampling of what is available. Librarians are encouraged to explore these sites and follow the links offered on each site to develop a comprehensive inventory of information sources on the Internet suited to the needs of their patrons who are looking for information and support related to disabilities and health issues.

ABLEDATA: THE NATIONAL DATABASE OF ASSISTIVE TECHNOLOGY INFORMATION
http://www.abledata.com
This extensive database lists information on assistive technology available both commercially and noncommercially from domestic and international manufacturers and distributors. It is excellent for practitioners, researchers, engineers, advocates, and consumers of rehabilitative and assistive technology.

ALL ABOUT HEALTH
http://www.allabouthealth.com/index.html
Comprehensive online magazine that offers several new articles on health each day and also has an impressive search feature called Healthlinx that provides links to hundreds of other health-related sites and organizations.

AMERICAN ACADEMY OF PEDIATRICS
http://www.aap.org/
This site's "You and Your Family" section offers a parent resource guide, a pediatric referral service, an immunization schedule, child care books, and updates on pediatric health issues.

AMERICAN ACADEMY OF CHILD & ADOLESCENT PSYCHIATRY
http://www.aacap.org/
Site for both professionals and parents that offers Breaking News, Facts

for Families, Journals and Publications, Clinical Practice, Managed Care and Public Health, Research, Training, and Meetings.

AMERICAN FOUNDATION FOR THE BLIND
http://www.igc.apc.org/afb/index.html
Offers viewers information on blindness; low vision and related issues; newsletters and press releases; the *Journal of Visual Impairment and Blindness* and other resources.

AMERICAN SOCIETY FOR DEAF CHILDREN
http://deafchildren.org
Organization of parents and families that advocates for deaf or hard-of-hearing children's total participation in education and the community. Offers membership information, resource materials, position papers, and much more.

THE ARC
http://thearc.org/
Web site of the country's largest voluntary organization committed to the welfare of all children and adults with mental retardation. This site offers fact sheets on topics related to mental retardation; state and local chapters; two different online newsletters relating to legislation affecting those with mental retardation; and position papers.

AskERIC and PARENTS AskERIC
http://ericps.ed.uiuc.edu//npin/paskeric.html
Parents AskERIC is an Internet-based information service that responds to questions on child development, child care, parenting, and child rearing. A response will generally include the results of a short search of the ERIC database and sometimes will include a referral to other Internet resources, a short list of other organizations or information providers that can be contacted for information, or the complete text of a relevant article.

ASSOCIATION FOR THE CARE OF CHILDREN'S HEALTH
http://look.net/ACCH/
Multidisciplinary organization of health care providers, facility designers, teachers, child life specialists, and families dedicated to improving the quality of health care for children. The Web site offers ACCH news; publications and resources; parent care; children and health care week; and links to other sites.

THE AUTISM CHANNEL
http://www.connect.net/sherman/access.html
A virtual newspaper created by parents and professionals featuring

several bulletin boards devoted to autism, links to other Internet sites, legislation updates, articles offering help to families, including the LOVASS method, the TEACCH method, behavior analysis, sensory integration therapy, and facilitated communication.

CHILDREN AND ADULTS WITH ATTENTION DEFICIT DISORDERS
http://www.chadd.org/
Parent-based organization site that offers attention deficit disorder information, government info, *Attention* magazine, membership information, CHADD online, and other resources.

COUNCIL FOR EXCEPTIONAL CHILDREN
http://www.cec.sped.org/home.htm
Professional organization's Web site whose features include public policy and legislative information, the ERIC Clearinghouse on Disabilities and gifted education, professional development events, CEC professional standards, a "what's new" section, and the National Clearinghouse for Professions in Special Education.

DIABETES MONITOR
http://www.mdcc.com/
A Web site devoted to people with diabetes. Offers searchable database, registry of Web links, hyperlinks to other diabetes sites, and a collection of brochures for families.

DISABILITY INFORMATION AND RESOURCES
http://www.eskimo.com/~jlubin/disabled/
Megasite that offers links to hundreds of other disability-related sites, databases, selected documents, and political groups.

DOWN SYNDROME WWW PAGE
http://www.nas.com/downsyn/
Compiled by members of the Down Syndrome Listserv, this home page provides information on Down syndrome and directs the user to other Down syndrome home pages, parent and sibling support groups, and disability and medical resources.

EPILEPSY FOUNDATION OF AMERICA (EFA)
http://www.efa.org/index1.htm
Jam-packed site that offers information and resources including Research, Epilepsy Information, Education, Advocacy, Kids' Korner, and the Gene Discovery Project.

FAMILY EDUCATION NETWORK
http://www.familyeducation.com/
Graphically interesting, comprehensive site offering daily features: School Time, Family Learning, Health and Safety, Activities, News Watch, Kidszone, Special Needs, Learning Disabilities, College and Homework Help.

FAMILY EMPOWERMENT NETWORK
http://www.downsydrome.com/
A graphically interesting, family-produced Web page devoted to empowering families of children with Down syndrome and other developmental disabilities. Offers Down syndrome WWW sites, Disability Solutions Newsletter, *Down Syndrome Online* magazine, government and medical resources, support groups for parents, and much more.

FAMILY VILLAGE: A GLOBAL COMMUNITY OF DISABILITY-RELATED RESOURCES
http://www.familyvillage.wisc.edu/
Web site maintained by the Waisman Center of the University of Wisconsin that offers a cornucopia of information categorized under 12 general menu options and opportunities to chat with other parents. Menu options are Library, Coffee Shop, Hospital, Shopping Mall, Post Office, House of Worship, School, Sports and Recreation, Community Center, Bookstore, University, and Information.

FAMILY VOICES
http://www.familyvoices.org
A Web site of a national organization of families and friends of children with special health needs. Offers statistics on numbers of children with special health needs, position papers, and listings of regional coordinators and national offices. Caveat for America Online users: Be sure to type address exactly as written; their browser is sensitive to letter case.

FRANK PORTER GRAHAM CHILD DEVELOPMENT CENTER
http://www.fpg.unc.edu/index.htm
Site of nationally recognized research center for the study of children at risk for developmental delays. Offers a listing of their projects, publications, and a "what's new" section.

HUMAN GROWTH FOUNDATION
http://www.genetic.org/hgf/
Offers information on dwarfism and other growth-related disorders, growth hormone treatments: what to expect, publications, and links.

INTERNATIONAL FEDERATION FOR HYDROCEPHALUS AND SPINA BIFIDA (IFHSB)

http://www.asbah.demon.co.uk/ifhsb.html

Organization that represents 30 national organizations for people living with hydrocephalus and spina bifida. Also offers information section, a newsletter online, and related links.

INTERNATIONAL RETT SYNDROME ASSOCIATION

http://www.paltech.com/irsa/irsa.htm

Organization devoted to helping girls afflicted with this syndrome and their families. Includes What Is Rett?, Living Image, RettNet Archive, happenings, publications, late-breaking news, research contacts, links, and much more.

INTERNET RESOURCES FOR SPECIAL CHILDREN

http://www.irsc.org/

Colorful Web page that offers a great disAbility links section. Twenty-six topics are offered—each has pages of links to other sites.

KIDS HEALTH ORGANIZATION WEB SITE

http://KidsHealth.org/index2.html

Nemours Foundation site that offers parents sections on general medicine and surgical health issues. Articles on asthma and allergies; bones and muscles; ear, nose, and throat; emergencies; fevers; growth and development; infection pain; sleep; and vaccines.

LEARNING DISABILITIES ASSOCIATION

http://www.ldanatl.org/

National organization's Web site that offers several resources for families including a comprehensive "Fact Sheets" section. Among the fact sheets offered are Central Auditory Processing Problems in Children, Dyslexia, and Early Identification of Speech and Language Disorders.

MARCH OF DIMES BIRTH DEFECTS FOUNDATION

http://www.modimes.org/

Organization dedicated to the prevention of birth defects offers a wealth of information and resources on such topics as having a healthy baby, birth defects information, infant health statistics, public and professional education, and their resource center home page.

MENTAL HEALTH NET

http://www.cmhc.com/

Comprehensive guide to 6,000 resources on mental health. Among its best offerings are the reading room and self-help resources where parents can access information and resources on problem areas and treatments.

MUSCULAR DYSTROPHY ASSOCIATION USA

http://www.mdausa.org/

Web site of organization with famous annual telethon that offers programs to assist persons with muscular dystrophy, forums for discussion, and an "Ask the Experts" feature.

NATIONAL HEALTH INFORMATION CENTER

http://nhic-nt.health.org/

Their Health Information Resource Database includes 1,100 organizations and government offices that provide health information upon request. Entries include contact information, short abstracts, and information about publications and services the organizations provide.

NATIONAL INFORMATION CENTER FOR CHILDREN AND YOUTH WITH DISABILITIES

http://nichcy.org/

Information and referral center for those involved with children with disabilities, ages birth to 22. Special features include state resource sheets, other disability clearinghouses, and publications in Spanish.

NEC*TAS

http://www.nectas.unc.edu/

Site of the National Early Childhood Technical Assistance System, the main support for every state's Part C programs under the Individuals with Disabilities Education Act. Offers an overview of NEC*TAS, NEC*TAS publications, meeting transcripts of the Federal Interagency Coordinating Council, selected Office of Special Education memoranda, a report on Part C, and a 619 briefing paper.

NATIONAL ORGANIZATION ON FETAL ALCOHOL SYNDROME (NOFAS)

http://www.nofas.org/

Includes a description of fetal alcohol syndrome, strategies to use with FAS children, FAS resources, and a description of NOFAS.

NATIONAL ORGANIZATION FOR RARE DISORDERS (NORD) RARE DISEASE DATABASE

http://www.raredisease.org

NORD maintains a Rare Disease database with information on hundreds of rare syndromes, diseases, and disorders. This information is often extremely difficult for parents to locate. Entries are written in simple, clear language so families can easily understand it. Includes description, symptoms, causes, related disorders, affected population, standard and investigational therapies, support groups, and sources of further information. The database is available online through

CompuServe (full texts of the articles can be downloaded through CompuServe). NORD can also be reached on the Internet at the World Wide Web address above but you will be charged $5 per article on specific diseases. If you do not have computer capability, you can contact NORD, PO Box 8923, New Fairfield, CT 06812–8923, (203) 746–6518, for reprints of their articles or further information.

NATIONAL REHABILITATION INFORMATION CENTER
http://www.cais.net/naric//index.html
A library and information center funded by the National Institute on Disability and Rehabilitation Research. Collects and disseminates the results of federally funded research projects. Collection is growing at a rate of over 250 documents per month.

NATIONAL SPINAL CORD INJURY ASSOCIATION
http://www.spinalcord.org/
Features articles, information, links, and support groups for persons living with spinal cord injuries.

NATIONAL TOURETTE SYNDROME ASSOCIATION INC.
http://neuro-www2.mgh.harvard.edu/TSA/TSAMAIN.NCLK
Offers description of organization (sponsored by Massachusetts General Hospital's Department of Neurology), facts about Tourette's syndrome, medical and scientific info, what's happening, and much more.

OUR KIDS
http://rdz.acor.org/lists/our-kids/
This Web page is devoted to raising kids with special needs and provides links to an array of disability-related news groups, databases, and home pages. Simple and friendly to use.

PARENTS HELPING PARENTS (PHP)
http://www.php.com/
PHP is a parent-directed family resource center for children with any kind of special need. This particular PHP Web site contains links to resources concerned with parenting and children with disabilities and medical conditions.

PEDINFO: An Index of the Pediatric Internet
http://WWW.UAB.EDU/pedinfo/
Provides access to condition or disease-specific information and resources for parents of children with special needs.

PROJECT PURSUIT
http://pursuit.rehab.uiuc.edu/pursuit/homepage.html

Disability-related site that has more than 400 pages of information and resources including career information for students with disabilities, employers seeking persons with disabilities as employees and access to other disability information servers.

RARE GENETIC DISEASES IN CHILDREN
http://mcrcr.med.nyu.edu/~murphp01/homenew/htm.
Comprehensive site that offers a searchable database, a worldwide messaging center, a resource directory, and much, much more.

SPECIAL EDUCATION RESOURCES ON THE INTERNET
http://www.hood.edu/seri/serihome.html
A collection of information resources for those involved in special education. Offers twenty-five pages of links on the following topics: legal and law resources, mental retardation, physical and health disorders, attention deficit disorder, speech impairments, inclusion resources, behavior disorders, and many other subjects.

UNITED CEREBRAL PALSY
http://www.ucpa.org/html/
A wealth of information on cerebral palsy and other disabilities. Menu choices include innovative projects, advocacy in action, research, fund raising, resource center, and discussion groups.

WIDESMILES
http://www.widesmiles.org
A cornucopia of information for families of children with cleft palates. Included are articles on cleft palates and related conditions, links to other sites, a quarterly newsletter, a guide to doctors and medical professionals, chat services, and a resource mall.

Internet resources are being developed on a daily basis and provide an extraordinary opportunity for families of children with disabilities. Librarians need to familiarize themselves with the sites that are particularly applicable for various audiences, including sources targeted to parents as well as children. Providing computers for in-library use and bookmarking appropriate sites helps families locate the information they need within the library setting. Publishing lists of Internet sites, offering courses on how to surf the Net, and selecting sites that are accessible from the library's home page helps both parents and children access the electronic information they need.

APPENDIX A: A BIBLIOGRAPHY OF PRINT AND AUDIOVISUAL MATERIALS

RESOURCES FOR PARENTS AND PROFESSIONALS

ABC's of Inclusive Child Care [videotape] Austin, TX: Texas Planning Council on Developmental Disabilities, 1993. 14 minutes; $^1/_2$" VHS.

Abraham, Marie R., Morris, Lori M., and Wald, Penelope J. *Inclusive Early Childhood Education: A Model Classroom*. Tucson, AZ: Communication Skill Builders, 1993.

Amado, Angela Novak, ed. *Friendships and Community Connections between People with and without Disabilities*. Baltimore: Paul H. Brookes, 1993.

Baker, Amy C. "New Frontiers in Family Day Care: Integrating Children With ADHD," *Young Children* 48, no. 5 (July 1993):69–73.

Blose, Dee A. and Smith, Laura L. *Thrifty Nifty Stuff for Kids: Developmental Play Using Home Resources*. Tucson, AZ: Communication Skill Builders, 1995.

Bricker, Diane E. and Cripe, Juliann Woods. *An Activity-Based Approach to Early Intervention*. Baltimore: Paul H. Brookes, 1992.

Brown, Wesley, Thurman, S. Kenneth, and Pearl, Lynda F., eds. *Family-Centered Early Intervention with Infants and Toddlers: Innovative Cross-Disciplinary Approaches*. Baltimore: P.H. Brookes, 1993.

Can I Play Too?: Overview [videotape] Chapel Hill, NC: Partnerships for Inclusion, Frank Porter Graham Child Development Center, University of North Carolina, 1993. 12 minutes; $^1/_2$" VHS.

Can I Play Too?: Parent Version [videotape] Chapel Hill, NC: Partnerships for Inclusion, Frank Porter Graham Child Development Center, University of North Carolina, 1993. 20 minutes; $^1/_2$" VHS.

Can I Play Too?: Provider Version [videotape] Chapel Hill, NC: Partnerships for Inclusion, Frank Porter Graham Child Development Center, University of North Carolina 1993. 20 minutes; $^1/_2$" VHS.

Caring for Children with Special Needs: The Americans with Disabilities Act and Child Care. San Francisco, CA: Child Care Law Center. Contact

Child Care Law Center, 22 Second Street, 5th Floor, San Francisco, CA 94105.

Chandler, Phyllis A. *A Place for Me: Including Children with Special Needs in Early Care and Education Settings.* Washington, D.C.: National Association for the Education of Young Children, 1994.

Child Care and the ADA: Highlights for Parents of Children with Disabilities. San Francisco, CA: Child Care Law Center, 1994. Contact the Child Care Law Center, 22 Second Street, 5th Floor, San Francisco, CA 94105.

Child Care and the Americans With Disabilities Act: Videotapes and Training Materials for Child Care Providers. [videotape set] Spokane, Wash.: Eastern Washington University. This set includes eight short videotapes on implementing inclusion in child care settings, including one tape specifically on family day care homes. Contact the Center for Technology, Education and the Community, Eastern Washington University, Paulsen Building, Suite 421, 407 Riverside, Spokane, WA 99201.

Child Care Plus+ : Supporting Inclusion in Early Childhood Settings. A newsletter published quarterly by the Rural Institute on Disabilities, University of Montana. To order a subscription ($5/yr.), contact Child Care Plus+, Rural Institute on Disabilities, Corbin Hall, University of Montana, Missoula, MT 59812, (800) 235–4122.

A Circle of Inclusion [videotape] Lawrence, KS: Learner Managed Designs, 1993. 27 minutes; $1/_2$" VHS. NOTE: Accompanied by a program guide, *A Circle of Inclusion: Facilitating the Inclusion of Young Children with Severe Disabilities.*

Coling, Marcia Cain. *Developing Integrated Programs: A Trans-Disciplinary Approach for Early Intervention.* Tucson, AZ: Therapy Skill Builder, 1991.

Cook, Ruth E. and Armbruster, Virginia. *Adapting Early Childhood Curricula: Suggestions for Meeting Special Needs.* St. Louis, MO: Mosby, 1987.

Cook, Ruth E., Tessier, Annette, and Klein, M. Diane. *Adapting Early Childhood Curricula for Children in Inclusive Settings.* Old Tappan, NJ: Macmillan, 1995.

Crawford, Jackie, et al. *Please! Teach All of Me: Multisensory Activities for Preschoolers.* Longmont, CO: Sopris West, 1994.

Derman-Sparks, Louise. *Anti-Bias Curriculum: Tools for Empowering Young Children.* Washington D.C.: National Association for the Education of Young Children, 1989.

Devine, Monica. *Growing Together: Communication Activities for Infants and Toddlers. Booklet 1: Birth to 12 Months; Booklet 2: 12 to 24 Months; Booklet 3: 24–36 Months.* Tucson, AZ: Communication Skill Builders, 1990.

Diversity Equals Inclusion [videotape] Bensenville, IL: National Easter Seal Society; 1994. 13 minutes; $1/_2$" VHS.

Doggett, Libby and George, Jill. *All Kids Count: Child Care and the Americans with Disabilities Act (ADA).* Arlington, TX: The ARC, 1993.

Dolinar, Kathleen J., et al. *Learning through Play: Curricula and Activities for the Inclusive Classroom.* Albany, NY: Delmar, 1994.

Early Childhood Education at Its Best [videotape] Mansfield, OH: North

Central Ohio Special Education Regional Resource Center, 1993. 30 minutes; $^1/_2$" VHS.

Exceptional Parent Magazine. Published monthly by the Psy-Ed Corporation. To order a subscription ($28/yr.), contact PO Box 3000, Dept. EP, Denville, NJ 07834, (800) 247–8080 or check your local library for availability.

Fauvre, Mary. "Including Young Children with 'New' Chronic Illnesses in an Early Childhood Education Setting," *Young Children* 43, no. 6 (September 1988): 71–77.

Fine, Aubrey H. and Fine, Nya M. *Therapeutic Recreation for Exceptional Children: Let Me In, I Want to Play.* Springfield, IL: Charles C. Thomas, 1988.

Friends Together: More Alike than Different [Poster Set] Fairless Hills, PA: Checkerboard Press, 1993. Set of twelve 11" x 17" color posters depicts young children with and without disabilities interacting in a variety of activities. Text by Rochelle Bunnett on each poster describes integrated early childhood activities appropriate for all children.

Friends Who Care: A Disability Awareness Program for Elementary Students [videotape] Chicago, IL: National Easter Seal Society, 1990. 45 minutes; $^1/_2$" VHS. Includes teacher's guide, attitude survey, posters, worksheets, and letter to parents.

Froschl, Merle, et al. *Including All of Us: An Early Childhood Curriculum about Disability.* New York: Educational Equity Concepts, 1984.

Grable, Trudy Marsh. "Integrated Neighborhood Playgroups: Creating an Environment Where Friendships Can Blossom," *Exceptional Parent* (July 1995): 44–46.

———. *Where Do I Begin? Integrated Neighborhood Playgroups.* Santa Clara, CA: PHP-The Family Resource Center, 1995.

Greenstein, Doreen, et al. *Backyards and Butterflies: Ways to Include Children with Disabilities in Outdoor Activities.* Ithaca, NY: New York State Rural Health and Safety Council, 1993.

Hackett, Louise Kennedy. *Everybody Belongs: Tips for Including Your Child in Community Recreation.* Concord, NH: New Hampshire Developmental Disabilities Council, 1994.

Hazel, Robin, et al. *A Community Approach to an Integrated Service Delivery System for Children with Special Needs.* Baltimore: Paul H. Brookes, 1988.

Hodge, Staisey. *Bright Ideas: Caring for Infants and Toddlers with Special Needs.* Little Rock, AR: Southern Early Childhood Association, 1995.

Inclusion: A Right, Not a Privilege. Farmington, CT: The Community Inclusion Project, Division of Child and Family Studies, Department of Pediatrics, University of Connecticut Health Center, n.d.

Klauber, Julie and Klauber, Avery. *Inclusion and Parent Advocacy: A Resource Guide.* Centereach, NY: Disability Resources, 1996.

LRE: A Policy of Inclusion (Early Childhood) [videotape] Fergus Falls, MN: West Central Educational Cooperative Service Unit. 23 minutes; $^1/_2$" VHS.

Mainstreaming in Child Care Settings: Helping Children Learn [videotape] Van Nuys, CA: Child Development Media, 1991. 25 minutes; $^1/_2$" VHS.

Mallory, Bruce L. and New, Rebecca S., eds. *Diversity and Developmentally Appropriate Practices: Challenges for Early Childhood Education.* New York: Teachers College Press, 1994.

Mapes, Marilyn K., Mapes, Jack C., and Ming-Gon, John Lian. *Education of Children with Disabilities from Birth to Three: A Handbook for Parents, Teachers, and Other Care Providers.* Springfield, IL: Charles C. Thomas, 1988.

McPhee, Norma H. *Sensitivity and Awareness: A Guide for Developing Understanding among Children,* Holidaysburg, PA: Jason & Nordic Publishers, 1994.

The More We Do Together: Adapting the Environment for Children with Disabilities. New York: World Rehabilitation Fund, 1985.

Morris, Lisa Rappaport and Schulz, Linda. *Creative Play Activities for Children with Disabilities: A Resource Book for Teachers and Parents.* Champaign, IL: Human Kinetics Books, 1989.

Mulligan, Sarah A., et al. *Integrated Child Care: Meeting the Challenge.* Tucson, AZ: Communication Skill Builders, 1992.

National Lekotek Center. Publishes many titles in support of inclusion and play opportunities for young children with disabilities, including *Lekotek Play Guide for Children with Special Needs; An Integrated Infant Play Group and Parent Support Curriculum: For Children from Birth to 12 Months Old; An Integrated Toddler Play Group and Parent Support Curriculum: For Children from 12–24 Months Old; An Integrated Play Group and Parent Support Curriculum: For Children from Two to Three Years of Age; An Early Childhood Play Group Curriculum for 3 to 5 Year Olds; Play Is a Child's World: A Lekotek Resource Guide on Play for Children with Disabilities for Family, Friends and Professionals; Come Play With Me! A Developmental Play Curriculum Guide for Teen Parents of Children from Birth to Three Years Old; Creating a Fully Accessible, Fantasy-Filled Halloween House for Children of All Abilities; Lekotek Plan Book of Adaptive Toys: Volume I, Volume II, Volume III.* These and several videos on infant stimulation, understanding disabilities, computer play, and toilet training are available from the National Lekotek Center, 2100 Ridge Avenue, Evanston, IL 60204, (708) 328–0001.

Neugebauer, Bonnie. *Alike and Different: Exploring Our Humanity with Young Children.* Washington, D.C.: National Association for the Education of Young Children, 1992.

NICHCY News Digest, publication of the National Information Center for Children and Youth with Disabilities. For a free subscription as well as many other free publications for parents and professionals on disabilities and disability-related issues, including a state-by-state listing of important resources, contact: NICHCY, PO Box 1492, Washington, D.C. 20013–1492, (800) 695–0285 or contact their Web site at http://www.aed.org/nichcy.

Nisbet, Jan, ed. *Natural Supports in School, at Work, and in the Community for People with Severe Disabilities.* Baltimore: Paul H. Brookes, 1992.

Odom, Samuel L., McConnell, Scott R., and McEvoy, Mary A., eds. *Social Competence of Young Children with Disabilities: Issues and Strategies for Intervention.* Baltimore: Paul H. Brookes, 1992.

Oregon Research Institute. *Child Care in the Neighborhood: Including Kids with Special Needs.* [videotape set] Tucson, AZ: Communication Skill Builders, 1995. Includes one video and one training manual.

Paasche, Carol L. et al. *Children with Special Needs in Early Childhood Settings.* Reading, MA: Addison-Wesley, 1990.

Parents' Vision of Inclusive Education [videotape] Niwot, CO: Expectations Unlimited, 1990. 67 minutes; $1/_2$" VHS.

Peck, Charles A., Odom, Samuel L., and Bricker, Diane D., eds. *Integrating Young Children with Disabilities into Community Programs: Ecological Perspectives on Research and Implementation.* Baltimore: Paul H. Brookes, 1993.

Perske, Robert and Perske, Martha. *Circles of Friends: People with Disabilities and Their Friends Enrich the Lives of One Another.* Nashville, TN: Abingdon Press, 1988.

Project Kidlink: Bringing Together Disabled and Nondisabled Preschoolers. Tucson, AZ: Communication Skill Builders, 1990.

Quilting Integration: A Technical Assistance Guide on Integrated Early Childhood Programs. Columbus, OH: Ohio State University, Center for Special Needs Population, 1993.

Rab, Victoria Y. *Child Care and the ADA: A Handbook for Inclusive Programs.* Baltimore: Paul H. Brookes, 1995.

Rogovin, Anne and Cataldo, Christine. *What's the Hurry? Developmental Activities for Able and Handicapped Children.* Baltimore: University Park Press, 1983.

Rose, Deborah F. and Smith, Barbara J. "Preschool Mainstreaming: Attitude Barriers and Strategies for Addressing Them," *Young Children* 48, no. 4 (May 1993): 59–62.

Ross, Helen Warren. "Integrating Infants with Disabilities? Can 'Ordinary' Caregivers Do It?," *Young Children* 47, no. 3 (March 1992):65–70.

Schwartz, Sue and Miller, Joan Heller. *The New Language of Toys: Teaching Communication Skills to Children with Special Needs.* Bethesda, MD: Woodbine House, 1996.

Searl, Julia, ed. *Serving Children with Special Needs in Your Child Care Facility.* Syracuse, NY: Early Childhood Inclusion Network of Onondaga County, 1996. Contact Early Childhood Direction Center, 805 South Crouse Avenue, Syracuse, NY 13244.

Segal, Marilyn. *In Time and with Love: Caring for the Special Needs Baby.* New York: Newmarket Press, 1988.

Sinker, Mary. *Toys for Growing: A Guide to Toys that Develop Skills.* Chicago: Year Book Medical Publishers for the National Lekotek Center in Evanston, IL, 1986.

Steele, Barbara. *Developing Community Networks: A Guide to Resources and Strategies.* Washington D.C.: Association for the Care of Children's Health, 1989.

Surr, John. "Early Childhood Programs and the Americans With Disabilities Act (ADA)," *Young Children* 47, no. 5 (July 1992): 18–21.

"Switches and Battery Interrupters Made Simple," *Exceptional Parent* 15 (November 1985): 64–65.

Taylor, Steven J., Bogdan, Robert, and Racino, Julie Ann, eds. *Life in the*

Community, Vol.1: Case Studies of Organizations Supporting People with Disabilities. Baltimore: Paul H. Brookes, 1991.

Thompson, Barbara et al. *Handbook for Inclusion of Young Children with Severe Disabilities: Strategies for Implementing Exemplary Full Inclusion Programs*. Lawrence, KS: Learner Managed Designs, 1993.

Turnbull, Ann P., Turnbull, H.R., and Blue-Banning, Martha. "Enhancing Inclusion of Infants and Toddlers with Disabilities and Their Families: A Theoretical and Programmatic Analysis," *Infants and Young Children* 7, no. 2 (October 1994): 1–14.

Turnbull, Rud and Turnbull, Ann. "Including All Children," *Children Today* 20, no. 2 (1991): 3–5.

Umstead, Serena, Boyd, Kimberly, and Dunst, Carl. "Building Community Resources: Enabling Inclusion in Community Programs and Activities," *Exceptional Parent* (July 1995): 36–37.

Van Den Pol, Richard, Guidry, Jean, and Keeley, Beth, eds. *Creating the Inclusive Preschool: Strategies for a Successful Program*. Tucson, AZ: Therapy Skill Builders, 1995.

Vaughn, Sharon and Rothlein, Liz. *Read It Again! Books to Prepare Children for Inclusion; Grades K-3*. Glenview, IL: GoodYear Books, Scott, Foresman and Co., 1994.

Webster, Elizabeth J. and Ward, Louise M. *Working with Parents of Young Children with Disabilities*. San Diego, CA: Singular Pub. Group, 1993.

Wesley, Patricia. *Mainstreaming Young Children: A Training Series for Child Care Providers*. Chapel Hill, NC: Frank Porter Graham Child Development Center, UNC-Chapel Hill, 1992.

White, Barbara Palm and Phair, Michael A. "It'll Be a Challenge!: Managing Emotional Stress in Teaching Disabled Children," *Young Children* 41, no. 2 (January 1986): 44–48.

Widerstrom, Anne H. *Achieving Learning Goals through Play*. Tucson, AZ: Communication Skill Builders, 1995.

Wolery, Mark and Wilbers, Jan S., eds. *Including Children with Special Needs in Early Childhood Programs*. Washington, D.C.: National Association for the Education of Young Children, 1994.

Wolfberg, Pamela J. and Schuler, Adriana L. *Integrated Play Groups Resource Manual*. San Francisco, CA: California Research Institute Project, 1992. Forty-five-minute video to accompany manual also available from California Research Institute Project, 14 Tapia Drive, San Francisco, CA 94132.

Wright, Christine and Nomura, Mari. *From Toys to Computers: Access for the Physically Disabled Child*. San Jose, CA: Christine Wright, 1987.

Yes, You Can Do It! Caring for Infants and Toddlers with Disabilities in Family Child Care. [videotape] Washington D.C.: The Children's Foundation, 1995. This videotape is accompanied by two publications: *Implications of the Americans with Disabilities Act of 1990 (ADA) for Family Child Care Providers* and *Caring for Infants and Toddlers with Disabilities in Family Child Care: Annotated Resource Directory*. Contact the Children's Foundation, 725 15th Street NW, Suite 505, Washington D.C. 20005-2109, (202) 347-3300.

ESPECIALLY FOR LIBRARIANS

Basu, S.G. *Public Library Services to Visually Disabled Children.* Jefferson, NC: McFarland and Company, 1991.

Crispen, Joanne L., ed. *Americans with Disabilities Act: Its Impact on Libraries: The Library's Responses in "Doable" Steps.* Chicago: American Library Association, 1993.

Deines-Jones, Courtney and Van Fleet, Connie. *Preparing Staff to Serve Patrons with Disabilities: A How-To-Do-It Manual for Librarians.* NY: Neal-Schuman, 1995.

Gross, Lois Rubin. "Handicapped Children in Library Programs," *Colorado Libraries* 14 (June 1988): 29.

Jackson, Sara. "A Puff of Breath, a Tilt of the Head and...Presto!...It's a Toy Library for Children with Disabilities," *Mississippi Libraries* 56, no. 3 (Fall 1992): 76–78.

Jackson, Sara C. "Toys, Not Books: A Special Youth Services Program," *Youth Services in Libraries* 9 (Winter 1996):199–201.

Klauber, Julie. "Toy Story: How to Select and Buy Adaptive Toys," *School Library Journal* 42, no. 7 (July 1996): 22–25.

Langa, Michelle A. and Feinberg, Sandra. "Implementing the Natural Environment of Part H With the Help of Children's Librarians," *Infants and Young Children: An Interdisciplinary Journal of Special Care Practices* 8, no. 4 (April 1996): 63–69.

Programming for Serving Children With Special Needs. Chicago: American Library Association, 1994.

"Story Hour at the Public Library: Ideas for Including Visually Impaired Preschoolers," fact sheet produced by National Library Service for the Blind and Physically Handicapped, The Library of Congress, Washington D.C. (June 1988).

Talcott, Anne E. "The Early Intervention Resources/Toy Lending Library: Helping 'At Risk' Toddlers and Their Parents," *Ohio Libraries* 4 (Jul/Aug 1991): 8–10.

Vaughn, Sharon and Rothlein, Liz. *Read It Again! Books to Prepare Children for Inclusion; Grades K-3.* Glenview, IL: GoodYear Books, Scott, Foresman and Co., 1994.

Velleman, Ruth A. *Meeting the Needs of People with Disabilities: A Guide for Librarians, Educators, and Other Service Professionals.* Phoenix, AZ: Oryx Press, 1990.

Walling, Linda Lucas and Irwin, Marilyn M. *Information Services for People with Developmental Disabilities: The Library Manager's Handbook.* Westport, CT: Greenwood Press, 1995.

Walling, Linda Lucas and Karrenbrock, Marilyn H. *Disabilities, Children, and Libraries: Mainstreaming Services in Public Libraries and School Library Media Centers.* Englewood, CO: Libraries Unlimited, 1993.

Wright, Kieth C. and Davis, Judith F. *Serving the Disabled: A How-To-Do-It Manual for Librarians.* New York: Neal Schuman, 1991.

BOOKS TO SHARE WITH YOUNG CHILDREN

Amenta, Charles A. *Russell Is Extra Special: A Book about Autism for Children*. New York: Magination Press, 1992.

Arnold, Katrin. *Anna Joins In*. Nashville, TN: Abingdon Press, 1982.

Brown, Tricia and Ortiz, Fran. *Someone Special, Just Like You*. New York: Holt, Rinehart and Winston, 1984.

Bunnett, Rochelle. *Friends at School*. New York: Star Bright Books, 1995.

————. *Friends in the Park*. New York: Checkerboard Press, 1992.

Caseley, Judith. *Harry and Willy and Carrothead*. New York: Greenwillow Books, 1991.

Cohen, Miriam. *See You Tomorrow, Charles*. New York: Greenwillow Books, 1983.

Dwight, Laura. *We Can Do It!* New York: Checkerboard Press, 1992.

Fassler, Joan. *Howie Helps Himself*. Chicago: Albert Whitman and Company, 1975.

Greenberg, Judith E. *What Is the Sign for Friend?* New York: Franklin Watts, 1985.

Greenfield, Eloise. *Darlene*. New York: Methuen, 1980.

Holcomb, Nan. *Andy Opens Wide*; *Cookie*; *Danny and the Merry-Go-Round*; *Fair and Square*; *How About a Hug*; *Patrick and Emma Lou*; *Sarah's Surprise*; *A Smile from Andy* (and other titles in the Turtle Books Series). Hollidaysburg, PA: Jason & Nordic Publishers. A workbook, entitled *Sensitivity and Awareness: A Guide for Developing Understanding among Children*, is also available from the publishers for parents and professionals to use in conjunction with the Turtle Books Series.

Kaufman, Curt and Kaufman, Gita. *Rajesh*. New York: Atheneum, 1985.

Kraus, Robert. *Leo the Late Bloomer*. New York: Windmill Books, 1971.

Lasker, Joe. *Nick Joins In*. Chicago: Albert Whitman and Company, 1980.

Levi, Dorothy Hoffman. *A Very Special Friend*. Washington, D.C.: Kendall Green Publications, 1989.

Litchfield, Ada B. *A Button in Her Ear*. Chicago: Albert Whitman and Company, 1976.

McMahon, Patricia. *Listen for the Bus: David's Story*. Honesdale, PA: Boyds Mills Press, 1995.

Moss, Deborah M. *Lee, The Rabbit With Epilepsy* and *Shelley, the Hyperactive Turtle*. Kensington, MD: Woodbine House, 1989.

Osofsky, Audrey. *My Buddy*. New York: Henry Holt, 1992.

Quinsey, Mary Beth. *Why Does That Man Have Such a Big Nose?* Seattle, WA: Parenting Press, 1986.

Rabe, Berniece. *Where's Chimpy?* Niles, IL: Albert Whitman and Company, 1988.

Rosenberg, Maxine B. *My Friend Leslie: The Story of a Handicapped Child*. New York: Lothrop, Lee and Shepard Books, 1983.

Russo, Marisabina. *Alex Is My Friend*. New York: Greenwillow Books, 1992.

Schwier, Karin Melberg. *Keith Edward's Different Day*. San Luis Obispo, CA: Impact Publishers, 1992.

Snell, Nigel. *Peter Gets a Hearing Aid*. London: Hamish Hamilton, 1979.

Stefanik, Alfred. *Copycat Sam: Developing Ties with a Special Child*. New York: Human Sciences Press, 1982.

Thompson, Mary. *My Brother Matthew*. Rockville, MD: Woodbine House, 1992.

Walker, Lou Ann. *Amy: The Story of a Deaf Child*. New York: Lodestar Books, 1985.

Watson, Esther. *Talking To Angels*. New York: Harcourt Brace and Company, 1996.

APPENDIX B: DEVELOPMENTAL MILESTONES FOR INFANTS AND YOUNG CHILDREN

A familiarity with developmental milestones is important for librarians when they design programs for young children or interact with parents who have questions and concerns about their child's behavior. This list, which provides some general characteristics associated with each state of development, has been culled from *Developmentally Appropriate Practice in Early Childhood Program Serving Children from Birth through Age Eight* by Sue Bredekamp (1987, Washington D.C.: National Association for Education of Young Children), and *A Family Child Care Provider's Guide to New York's Early Intervention Program: Trainer's Manual* (1996, Albany, N.Y.: Early Intervention Program, New York State Department of Health).

1 to 3 months
Lifts head and chest briefly when on stomach
Turns head toward bright colors and lights
Eyes follow moving object with both eyes moving in the same direction
Pays attention to someone's face in his or her direct line of vision
Reacts to sudden sounds and noises
Smiles and coos
Makes fist with both hands; can grasp toys or hair
Wiggles and kicks with arms and legs

3 to 6 months
Follows moving objects with eyes
Recognizes familiar faces and objects
Turns toward sounds
Turns over from back to stomach
Stretches out arms to be picked up
Babbles and laughs out loud
Reaches for and holds objects; can switch toys from one hand to the other
Helps hold bottle during feeding

6 to 12 months

Sits without support
Pulls to a standing position
Creeps or crawls
Finger-feeds self; drinks from a cup
Plays peekaboo and patty cake; waves bye-bye
Looks at person speaking
Uses crying to show different needs
Responds to name; pats and smiles at image in mirror
Knows strangers from family
Uses five or six words including "mama" and "dada"
Holds out arms and legs while being dressed
Picks up objects with thumb and forefinger and looks closely at them; puts objects in containers
Stacks two blocks

12 to 18 months

Pushes, pulls, and dumps things
Pulls off shoes, socks, and mittens
Walks with help
Steps off a low object and keeps balance
Follows simple directions (e.g., "Bring the ball," "Give it to me," "Stop!")
Imitates simple words
Likes to listen to music and dance in rhythm to it
Likes to look at pictures
Tries to build and stack objects
Feeds himself or herself
Makes marks on paper with crayon

18 to 24 months

Carries something while walking
Feeds self with a spoon
Refers to self by name
Turns pages two or three at a time
Listens to stories with pictures
Uses two-to-three word sentences
Has a vocabulary of 300 words
Says names of toys
Carries on "conversations" with self and dolls
Builds a tower of four blocks
Recognizes familiar pictures
Plays independently for short periods of time
Imitates parents and everyday activities
Identifies hair, eyes, ears, and nose by pointing

Shows affection
Beginning to run and jump
Likes to scribble and draw
Puts squares and circles into puzzles

24 to 30 months
Kicks a ball
Turns pages one at a time
Can help to dress and undress
Turns doorknob and unscrews lids
Feeds self well with spoon
Uses many new words
Speaks in short sentences
Names objects in books
Pays attention to activities for longer periods of time (6–7 minutes)
Knows at least one color
Points to parts of body

30 to 36 months
Walks up stairs (alternating feet)
Rides a tricycle
Puts on shoes
Plays with other children for short periods of time
Repeats common nursery rhymes
Says first and last name
Knows whether he/she is a boy/girl
Follows two- or three-step directions given at one time
Begins to count
Begins to draw circles and vertical lines
Uses three- to five-word sentences
Has vocabulary of 1,000 words
Uses works to relate observations, concepts, and relationships
Understands night/day, big/little, summer/winter, yesterday/today
Can stay with one activity for 8–9 minutes

36 to 48 months
Speaks in short sentences within a context of conversation
Asks many how, why, when, what, and where questions
Gradually replaces parallel play with cooperative play
Opens and turns pages of a book
Knows the front and back of a book; can recognize if book is up-
 side down
Likes to hear the same story over and over again
Listens to a book with a very simple storyline
Counts using a one-to-one correspondence

Builds a tower with nine blocks
Begins to draw a stick-figure person
Is toilet trained and able to use restrooms with assistance
Is able to dress and undress independently
Is able to put toys or materials away when asked

48 to 60 months
Has a vocabulary of about 1,500 words
Understands spatial language (over, under, in, out)
Actively engages in conversations with other children
Follows directions requiring sequential order
Orders objects by size, number, shape
Begins to recognize colors, numbers, and letters
Strings beads in a pattern
Begins to use scissors
Engages in more elaborate and sophisticated dramatic play
Follows a story with a full storyline
Sits in a group for 15 or more minutes
Separates from parent or caregiver for a short period of time

APPENDIX C: PART C (INDIVIDUALS WITH DISABILITIES EDUCATION ACT) COORDINATORS

The Individuals with Disabilities Education Act (IDEA) authorizes the states to provide service to young children with disabilities. Part C of IDEA addresses interventions for infants and toddlers under the age of three. The following list serves as a guide to librarians who wish to make contact with their state's coordinator of early intervention and special preschool services. These contacts can provide information on the state's system and a listing of local contacts.

Part C Coordinator
Division of Rehabilitative Services, CCS
2129 E. South Boulevard
P.O. Box 11586
Montgomery, Alabama 36111–0586

Program Coordinator
Dept. of Health and Social Services
1231 Gambell Street
Anchorage, Alaska 99501–4627

Interagency Coordinating Council for Infants and Toddlers
Arizona Dept. of Economic Security
1717 W. Jefferson, Room 109
P.O. Box 6123 Site Code (801A-6)
Phoenix, Arizona 85005

Part C Coordinator
Division of Developmental Disabilities
Dept. of Human Services
Donaghey Plaza North
7th and Main Streets
P.O. Box 1437, Slot 2520
Little Rock, Arkansas 72203–1437

Part C Coordinator
Community Services Division
Dept. of Developmental Services
P.O. Box 944202
Sacramento, California 95815

Part C Coordinator
Special Education Division
State Dept. of Education
201 E. Colfax Street
Denver, Colorado 80203

Part C Coordinator
Early Childhood Unit
Bureau of Curriculum and Professional Development
25 Industrial Park Road
Middletown, Connecticut 06455

Part C Coordinator
Dept. of Health and Social Services
1901 N. Dupont Highway—Main Building
New Castle, Delaware 19720

Part C Coordinator
Dept. of Health and Rehabilitation Services
Children's Medical Services
1317 Winewood Boulevard, Building B
Tallahassee, Florida 32399–0700

Part C Coordinator
Division of Public Health
Dept. of Human Resources
Babies Can't Wait Program
2 Peachtree Street NE 7th Floor
Atlanta, Georgia 30303

Project Director
Zero to Three Hawaii
Children with Special Health Needs
Family Health Services Division, Dept. of Health
1600 Kapiolani Boulevard, Suite 925
Honolulu, Hawaii 96814

Part C Coordinator
Infant Toddler Program
Dept. of Health and Welfare
Tower Office Building
4450 W. State Street, 7th Floor
Boise, Idaho 83720

Part C Coordinator
Special Education Dept.
100 West Rudolph
C-14300
Chicago, Illinois 60601

Part C Coordinator
Division on Developmental Disabilities
Dept. of Mental Health
412 W. Washington Street W-386
Indianapolis, Indiana 46204

Part C Coordinator
c/o University of Northern Iowa
133 Education Center
Cedar Falls, Iowa 50614

Part C Coordinator
Infant and Toddler Service
Bureau for Children, Youth, and Families
Dept. of Health and Environment,
Landon State Office Building
900 SW Jackson, 10th Floor
Topeka, Kansas 66612–1290

Part C Coordinator
Division of Mental Retardation
Dept. of Mental Health and Mental Retardation
275 E. Main Street
Frankfort, Kentucky 40621

Part C Coordinator
Office of Special Education Services
State Dept. of Education
P.O. Box 94064
Baton Rouge, Louisiana 70804–9064

Part C Coordinator
Child Development Services
87 Winthrop Street
State House Station 146
Augusta, Maine 04333

Director
Prevention and Early Intervention for Young Children
One Market Center, Suite 304
300 W. Lexington Street, Suite 15
Baltimore, Maryland 21201

Director of Early Childhood Unit
Developmental Services Unit
Division of Family Health Services
Dept. of Public Health
150 Tremont Street, 7th Floor
Boston, Massachusetts 02111

Part C Coordinator
Early Childhood Education
State Dept. of Education
P.O. Box 30008
Lansing, Michigan 48909

Part C Coordinator
Interagency Planning Project for Young Children with Handicaps
835 Capitol Square Building
550 Cedar Street
Street Paul, Minnesota 55101

Part C Coordinator
Children's Medical Programs
State Board of Health
P.O. Box 1700
2423 N. State Street, Room 105A
Jackson, Mississippi 39215–1700

Part C Coordinator
Section of Special Education
Dept. of Elementary and Secondary Education
P.O. Box 480
Jefferson City, Missouri 65102

Part C Coordinator
Management Operations Bureau
Developmental Disabilities Division
Dept. of Social and Rehabilitation Services
P.O. Box 4210
Helena, Montana 59604–4210

Part C Coordinator
Special Education Office
State Dept. of Education
P.O. Box 94987
Lincoln, Nebraska 68509

Part C Coordinator
Dept. of Human Resources
Office of the Director
3987 S. McCarran Boulevard
Air Center Plaza
Reno, Nevada 89502

Part C Coordinator
New Hampshire Infant and Toddler Project
Division of Mental Health and Mental Retardation
Dept. of Health and Human Services
105 Pleasant Street
Concord, New Hampshire 03301

Part C Coordinator
Special Child Health Services
Dept. of Health
363 W. State Street (CN364)
Trenton, New Jersey 08625–0364

Part C Coordinator
Developmental Disabilities Bureau
Dept. of Health
Harold Runnel Building
1190 Street Francis Drive
P.O. Box 26110
Sante Fe, New Mexico 87502–6110

Part C Coordinator
State of New York Dept. of Health Early Intervention Program
Bureau of Child and Adolescent Health
Empire State Plaza
Corning Tower
Albany, New York 12237–0618

Chief of Day Services
Developmental Disabilities Section
Dept. of Human Resources
325 N. Salisbury Street, Room 1156
Raleigh, North Carolina 27603

Part C Coordinator
Developmental Disabilities Division
Dept. of Human Resources
600 E. Boulevard Avenue
Bismarck, North Dakota 58505–0270

Part C Coordinator
Early Intervention Program, Division of Maternal, Child Health
Dept. of Health
P.O. Box 118
246 N. High Street, 4th Floor
Columbus, Ohio 43266–0118

Early Intervention Coordinator
Oklahoma Commission for Child and Youth
State Dept. of Education
Oliver Hodge Memorial Education Building, 4th Floor
2500 N. Lincoln Boulevard
Oklahoma City, Oklahoma 73105–4599

Coordinator of Early Intervention Program
Dept. of Education
700 Pringle Parkway, SE
Salem, Oregon 97301

Part C Coordinator
Office of Mental Retardation
Health and Welfare Building, Room 412
P.O. Box 2675
Harrisburg, Pennsylvania 17105–2675

Part C Coordinator
Dept. of Health
Division of Family Health
Room 302 Cannon Building
3 Capitol Hill
Providence, Rhode Island 02908–5097

Part C Coordinator
Division of Children's Health
Dept. of Health and Environmental Control
Robert Mills Complex
Box 101106
Columbia, South Carolina 29201

Part C Coordinator
Section for Special Education
Division of Education
Dept. of Education and Cultural Affairs
Kneip Building
700 Governors Drive
Pierre, South Dakota 57501

Part C Coordinator
Office for Special Education
State Dept. of Education
710 James Robertson Parkway
8th Floor, Gateway Plaza
Nashville, Tennessee 37243–0380

Administrator
Early Childhood Intervention Program
Dept. of Health
1100 W. 49th Street
Austin, Texas 78756–3199

Part C Coordinator
Family Health Services
Dept. of Health
P.O. Box 144620
Salt Lake City, Utah 84114–4620

Part C Coordinator, Children with Special Needs
Dept. of Health
108 Cherry Street
P.O. Box 70
Burlington, Vermont 05402

Part C Coordinator
Early Intervention Program
109 Governor Street, 10th Floor
P.O. Box 1797
Richmond, Virginia 23214

Part C Coordinator
Office of the Commissioner
Dept. of Human Services
609 H Street, NE 4th Floor
Washington, D.C. 20002

Part C Coordinator
Birth to Six Planning Project
Dept. of Social and Health Services
12th and Franklin Streets
P.O. Box 45201
Olympia, Washington 98504–5201

Part C Coordinator
Early Intervention
1116 Quarrier Street
Charleston, West Virginia 25301

Birth to Three Coordinator
State of Wisconsin
Dept. of Health and Social Services
Division of Community Services
One W. Wilson Street
Room 531, P.O. Box 7851
Madison, Wisconsin 53707

Part C Coordinator
Developmental Disabilities Division
Herchler Building
1413 1st Floor West
Cheyenne, Wyoming 82002

APPENDIX D:
THE NEW YORK STATE DEVELOPMENTAL DISABILITIES PLANNING COUNCIL'S LIBRARY-BASED PARENT RESOURCE CENTER INITIATIVE

This appendix describes the experiences of the New York State Developmental Disabilities Planning Council's (DDPC) Library-Based Parent Resource Center initiative, including lessons learned during project implementation and evaluation and a listing of libraries participating in the project.

The New York State Developmental Disabilities Planning Council, with the assistance of the New York State Education Department's Division of Library Development, funded a series of eleven parent resource centers in public libraries across New York State to serve the needs of families, especially families of children with special needs. Six libraries received minigrants for a twelve-month period; two individual libraries and three regional systems received larger grants for eighteen months. Because the larger grants supported multiple sites, a total of nineteen library-based parent resource centers serving diverse populations were developed.

Middle Country Public Library in Centereach, New York, conducted training institutes for libraries participating in these grants. The Middle Country Parent/Child Workshop model was established in 1979 and had a long history of serving families. It has been replicated throughout New York State as well as in other libraries nationwide. This exemplary program was one of the core programs adopted by several of the DDPC project participants and was recognized by the New York State Task Force on Child Abuse and Neglect as a primary prevention program and by the New York State Department of Health as an early intervention program. It is noted in several major publications, including Ellin Greene's *Books, Babies and Libraries* (Chicago: American Library Association, 1991) and Denny Taylor's *Many Families*

Many Literacies (New York: Heinemann, 1997), and, most recently, it was targeted as a core program for replication through the Hasbro Children's Foundation "Family Place" grant under the auspices of Middle Country Public Library and Libraries for the Future. The program is described in detail in *Running a Parent/Child Workshop: A How-To-Do-It Manual for Librarians* by S. Feinberg and K. Deerr (New York: Neal-Schuman, 1995).

As evidenced by the variety of approaches taken by the participating libraries in the DDPC project, each library established its own unique parent resource center in a way that furthered its organizational mission, responded to local needs, and built on its own institutional and community strengths.

The major services of library-based parent resource centers developed in the DDPC sites include access to a special collection of print and nonprint materials, educational programs ranging from interactive workshops for parents and children to seminars for parents, and information and referral services to link families to community-based service providers. Each library's offerings reflected community need as well as the availability of library and community resources but all created or strengthened their parenting collections and increased their informational materials about community service providers. Some DDPC centers chose to relocate or renovate collection space. Parents and community volunteers assisted in preparing the space while Friends groups and other local organizations donated materials.

LESSONS LEARNED

The New York State experience validates the development of library-based programs and collections to help parents and professionals obtain information on pregnancy, parenting, child development, and developmental disabilities in young children. It confirms that through the establishment of parent resource centers, libraries strengthen collaborative efforts with community service agencies and advocacy groups, and increase positive visibility and support for libraries.

IMPROVED INFORMATION ACCESS FOR PARENTS

Participating DDPC libraries were asked to improve and expand their collection of materials on child development, childhood disabilities, prevention, and early intervention. This meant discarding old and outdated items, purchasing more current materials, and shelving them in a prominent place in the library. Collections included multimedia materials and computer programs as well as print resources. Videotapes, low literacy resources, and materials in languages other than English were often the most used materials in the collection although low literacy and foreign language materials were also the most challenging to locate. Some libraries established electronic "discussion groups" through a computer network to connect parents with area professionals. They found that through electronic bulletin boards and online sources, parents were able to share concerns and get a wealth of information.

INCREASED LIBRARY USE THROUGH COLLABORATION

Along with making sure that these materials were available, the libraries worked with other organizations and advocacy groups in the community to reach families who didn't ordinarily go to the library. They developed special workshops and programs for families on child development. These programs presented information on what to do and where to go when it was thought that a child or family might need assistance or services. In some instances, health and child development screening programs were held at the library. Librarians began working closely with professionals and community organizations to improve the information that was available for families at the library and other places in the community.

As a result, library staff and community agencies reported an increase in use of the library by parents overall and particularly by members of each library's target audience. Local target audiences included expectant parents, parents of children with developmental delays and disabilities, children with special needs and their siblings, caregivers, low income families, parents with low literacy skills or whose home language was other than English, as well as the professionals working with these groups. Libraries reported the most difficulty in reaching pregnant and parenting teenagers.

MORE POSITIVE IMAGE OF LIBRARY IN THE COMMUNITY

Parent comments were very positive when asked about the parent resource centers and the programs, resources, and workshops they offered. They reported receiving new information, feeling less isolated, and enjoying uninterrupted time with their children. Several libraries elected to institute the parent/child workshop as one of their primary project activities. Library and community agency personnel noticed that parents who had participated in the parent/child workshop learned skills to improve their way of relating to their children. Parents also were introduced to child development specialists and other community service providers in various ways. These strategies included meeting professionals at library-sponsored workshops, through brochures and print or computerized resource directories developed by or available at the library, and by talking with other parents. A community survey showed that the parents who used the library for parenting materials or workshops tended to become more frequent library users.

The libraries involved in this project reported on the transformational effect of their work. In all instances, the relationship between libraries and community agencies improved. New partnerships with community agencies led libraries to become more integral to the local and regional community and family services system. Some community agencies began working with libraries on staff training as well as a support and complement to direct services. Often this meant more work for library personnel. Unanimously, the involved personnel agreed that the outcomes for families and communities were well worth the extra effort.

EFFECT ON PARTICIPATING LIBRARIES

The development of these parent resource centers encouraged participating libraries to look at issues that had an impact on their ability to serve the community. These issues included physical accessibility for individuals with disabilities and parents with infants and toddlers; staffing and specialization; program content; and support services like transportation and child care. Not surprisingly, the parent resource centers generated new funds or resources that benefitted both the resource center and the entire library. Sometimes, these were in the form of grants and cash gifts but more often it was in the form of generous donations of time or materials.

REPLICATION

The New York Library Association assisted the DDPC in encouraging more libraries to replicate these programs in their communities. The strategies, lessons, and experiences described in this chapter were identified in B. P. Cohen and L. S. Simkin's *Evaluation of the Implementation and Early Outcomes of Library-Based Parent Resource Centers* (Albany: New York State Developmental Disabilities Planning Council and New York Library Association, 1994) and set forth in B. P. Cohen and L. S. Simkin's *Library-Based Parent Resource Centers: A Guide to Implementing Programs* (Albany: New York State Developmental Disabilities Planning Council and New York Library Association, 1995), a guide to help libraries implement resource center programs. Additional information can be found in The *Resource Guide to Evaluation of Developmental Disability Planning Council Grant*

Projects by E. Carter (Albany: New York State Education Department, Division of Library Development, 1993).

CONCLUSION

DDPC found libraries and library personnel to be creative and enthusiastic partners in serving the information needs of families in their communities. While the development of a parent resource center in a community library takes time, energy, resources, and commitment, the DDPC-funded, library-based parent resource centers demonstrated the positive impact on patrons, the library, and the community. In meeting the information needs of families, participating libraries significantly enhanced their visibility, prestige, and support within their communities. Parent resource center staff were unanimous in saying the benefits to families, library, and community were well worth the work that went into establishing their parent resource centers.

DDPC DEMONSTRATION PARENT RESOURCE CENTERS

TRAINERS
Middle Country Public Library
101 Eastwood Boulevard
Centereach, NY 11720
Phone: (516) 585–9393

MINIPROJECTS
Groton Public Library
112 E. Cortland Street
Groton, NY 13073
Phone: (607) 898–5055

Lancaster Public Library
5466 Broadway
Lancaster, NY 14086
Phone: (716) 683–1120

Lyons School District Public Library
67 Canal Street
Lyons, NY 14489
Phone: (315) 946–9262

Mastic-Moriches-Shirley Community Library
301 William Floyd Parkway
Shirley, NY 11967
Phone (516) 399–1511

Newburgh Free Library
124 Grand Street
Newburgh, NY 12550
Phone: (914) 561–1985

Sand Lake Town Library
P.O. Box 363
West Sand Lake, NY 12196
Phone: (518) 674–5050

LARGE PROJECTS
Brooklyn Public Library
Grand Army Plaza
Brooklyn, NY 11238
Phone: (718) 780–7712

Crandall Public Library
251 Glen Street, City Park
Glens Falls, NY 12801
Phone: (518) 792–1509

Mid-Hudson Library System
103 Market Street
Poughkeepsie, NY 12601
Phone: (914) 471–6060

Onondaga County Public Library
The Galleries of Syracuse
447 S. Salina Street
Syracuse, NY 13202
Phone: (315) 448–4700

Port Washington Public Library
One Library Drive
Port Washington, NY 11050
Phone: (516) 883–4400

INDEX

ABOUT THE AUTHORS

Sandra Feinberg has devoted the past 25 years to public library service. It is this experience that she brings to her present position as director of the Middle Country Public Library (Centereach, N.Y.). Feinberg is an advocate for improving the quality of life for children and families, oversees a district of 56,000 people that circulates more than 1,200,000 items annually and operates with a current budget of over $7 million. A passionate believer in the ability of public libraries to be family-oriented community institutions, she has been a frontrunner in the development of innovative programs and services for children and parents. In collaboration with many colleagues in other disciplines, Feinberg founded the Suffolk Coalition for Parents and Children in 1980. This organization has grown into a network of over 1,500 professionals, still providing ongoing opportunities for education, advocacy, and information sharing on behalf of children and families on a bimonthly basis. Feinberg continues to be a leader in the development of programs and services for public libraries. She is the co-author of *Running a Parent/Child Workshop: A How-To-Do-It Manual for Librarians* (Neal-Schuman, 1995); *Serving Families and Children through Partnerships: A How-to-Do-It Manual for Librarians* (Neal-Schuman, 1996); *Parenting Bibliography* (Scarecrow, 1994); and *Learning Environments for Young Children: Rethinking Library Spaces and Services* (ALA Editions, 1998). Feinberg is currently an adjunct professor at the Palmer School of Library and Information Science, Long Island University. She lives in Stony Brook, N.Y., with her husband and two sons.

Barbara Jordan is head of Parenting and Clearinghouse Services for the Middle Country Public Library (Centereach, N.Y.). She is responsible for the development of a comprehensive, multimedia resource center for parents and professionals working with families and children. She is a leader in the field of parent education, cofounder of the local Parent Educator's Network and board member of the Family Resource Coalition of New York State. Jordan administered the Partners for Inclusion Project at Middle Country, a project aimed at improving opportunities for the inclusion of children with disabilities in community settings. The author of numerous publications to increase access to information for parents and family serving professionals, Jordan is co-author of *Audiovisual Resources for Family Programming* (New York: Neal-Schuman, 1994); *A Family Child Care Provider's Guide to New York's Early Intervention Program* (Albany, N.Y.: New York State Department of Health, 1996); *Partners for Inclusion: Welcoming Infants and Toddlers with Disabilities and Their Families into Community Activities: A Replication Guide* (Hauppauge,

N.Y.: Suffolk County Department of Health, 1997); and a contributor to *Serving Families and Children through Partnerships: A How-To-Do-It-Manual for Librarians* (Feinberg, S. and S. Feldman, New York: Neal-Schuman, 1996). Jordan has a degree in sociology from Adelphi University and an M.L.S. from Queens College. She has two grown sons and lives in Coram, N.Y., with her husband.

Kathleen Deerr has worked with children and families for over 20 years and is the assistant director in charge of the Children's and Parent's Services Department of the Mastics-Moriches-Shirley Community Library (Shirley, N.Y.). Recognizing early on that a child's most important role models and teachers are parents and caregivers, she has developed many innovative, interdisciplinary programs that focus on parent/caregiver and child interactions. She is actively involved in the development of model library-based programs for children with special needs. She is the co-author with Feinberg of *Running a Parent/ Child Workshop: A How-To-Do-It Manual For Librarians*. Other publications include numerous journal articles as well as contributions to the Bowker publication, *Play Learn and Grow*, and the ALA publication, *Youth Services Librarians As Managers: A How-To Guide from Budgeting to Personnel*. A lifelong advocate for children, Deerr has presented numerous workshops and lectures on the role of the public library in serving and supporting children and families as well as lectures on the administration and management of childrens' and parents' services in public libraries. She lives in West Hampton, N.Y., with her husband and son.

Michelle A. Langa, M.P.A., C.A.S., is an educator with more than twenty-five years' experience in the field of special education. She is presently employed as the director of special education for the Hampton School District in New Hampshire. In the past, Michelle held several administrative positions as the executive director of three different agencies serving children with special needs, the director of special education for a large school district and as the executive director of a multisite preschool and child care center. As a consultant, Michelle has developed three training curricula (one with Feinberg and Jordan) for New York State's Early Intervention Program; one of which was developed in collaboration with *Mister Rogers' Neighborhood*. She has also published several online articles for LRPNET and Parenthoodweb.com as well as articles for clinical journals. She lives in Durham, N.H., with her husband, daughter, and son.